About the Authors

Sheila Anne Dean, M.S., CCC-SLP, received a Bachelor's Degree from Ohio University and a Master's Degree from Miami University. She has worked for more than ten years in the public schools as a speech pathologist and a speech pathologist supervisor. Her role as a speech pathologist includes collaboration with teachers, parents, and other support staff while working with students individually, in small groups, and in the classroom setting. Previous presentations have included incorporating reading skills into therapy for school success, aligning instruction to meet classroom expectations, designing effective IEPs, and enhancing communication skills for at-risk and disabled children.

Jeri Lynn Fox, M.S., holds a Bachelor of Arts Degree from Bluffton College and a Master of Science Degree from the University of Dayton. A Martha Holden Jennings scholar, she has worked in public education for more than twenty-five years as a classroom teacher and school counselor. In her current role as school counselor, her responsibilities include improving student achievement, assessment coordination, and developing supportive parent/teacher partnerships and programming.

Pamela B. Meggyesy, M.A., earned a Bachelor of Science Degree in Education and a Master of Arts Degree in literature from Ohio University. Additionally, she has studied at Oxford University in Oxford, England. A thirty-year veteran classroom teacher in public schools, she has been involved with curriculum alignment and literature selection at the district and county levels. Additionally, she has chaired a district-wide writing initiative for her school system. She also has been an instructor at Wright State University.

Pamela Marie Thompson, M.S., has a Master's Degree in counseling from Wright State University and a Master's Degree in school psychology from the University of Dayton. She has taught at the college level and worked as a counselor and program director for a mental health clinic where she supervised case managers and a partial hospitalization program. She is currently employed as a school psychologist. Her background includes experience in testing, assessment, and academic intervention. She has worked in this field for eighteen years. An often sought-after speaker, she has presented numerous workshops dealing with a variety of educational topics including program evaluation, reading comprehension skill development, behavioral interventions, problem-solving skills, a concurrent session on instructional planning for the inclusive classroom at the Ohio School Psychologists Association state conference, sessions on teaching critical-thinking skills for the Association of School Administrators in Washington State, and the International Reading Association.

The authors have worked together for more than a decade in the Northridge School District in Dayton, Ohio. Their varied educational backgrounds and experiences bring a multifaceted approach to their collaborative educational projects.

© 2006 Englefield & Associates, Inc.

Acknowledgements

Show What You Know® Publishing acknowledges the following for their efforts in making this assessment material available for students, parents, and teachers.

Cindi Englefield, President/Publisher
Eloise Boehm-Sasala, Vice President/Managing Editor
Lainie Burke Rosenthal, Project Editor/Graphic Designer
Erin McDonald, Project Editor
Christine Filippetti, Project Editor
Jill Borish, Project Editor
Charles V. Jackson, Project Editor
Heather Holliday, Project Editor
Jennifer Harney, Illustrator/Cover Designer

For Grade 6

Student Workbook

Read on Target

This Book Belongs To: Kaitlin

Using Reading Maps to Improve Reading Comprehension and to Increase Critical-Thinking Skills

Written By:
Sheila Anne Dean, M.S., CCC-SLP
Jeri Lynn Fox, M.S.
Pamela B. Meggyesy, M.A.
Pamela Marie Thompson, M.S.

Show What You Know® Publishing

Published By:
Show What You Know® Publishing
A Division of Englefield & Associates, Inc.
P.O. Box 341348
Columbus, OH 43234-1348
1-877-PASSING (727-7464)

www.showwhatyouknowpublishing.com

Copyright © 2006 by Englefield & Associates, Inc.

All rights reserved. No part of this book, including interior design, cover design, and icons, may be reproduced or transmitted in any form, by any means (electronic, photocopying, recording, or otherwise), without the prior written permission of the publisher.

Printed in the United States of America
08 07 06   20 19 18 17 16 15 14 13 12 11 10 9 8 7 6 5 4 3 2

ISBN: 1-59230-153-3

Limit of Liability/Disclaimer of Warranty: The authors and publishers have used their best efforts in preparing this book. Englefield & Associates, Inc., and the authors make no representation or warranties with respect to the contents of this book and specifically disclaim any implied warranties and shall in no event be liable for any loss of any kind including but not limited to special, incidental, consequential, or other damages.

Dedication

To our families:

David, Sarah, Marie, Elaine, and Erin, thanks for your love.
Because of you, I truly "enjoy every day." –SAD

Richard, Amy, and Anna, thank you for the joy you bring to my life. –JLF

Joe, Mark, and Lauren; I treasure each of you. –PBM

Nathan, Olivia, and Jason, thanks for your love and encouragement. –PMT

and

To our first teachers:
our parents, by birth and by marriage,
with love and appreciation:

George and Carolyn Harrington and Carl and Marianna Dean –SAD

Charles and Edith Harlow and Richard and Janice Fox –JLF

George and Connie Besuden –PBM

Joe and Emily and Harold and Marie –PMT

Table of Contents

Introduction vii

Activity 1: Analyze Aspects of the Text by Examining Characters 1

Activity 2: Analyze Aspects of the Text by Examining Setting 7

Activity 3: Analyze Aspects of the Text by Examining Plot 13

Activity 4: Analyze Aspects of the Text by Examining Problem/Solution 19

Activity 5: Analyze Aspects of the Text by Examining Point of View 25

Activity 6: Analyze Aspects of the Text by Examining Theme 31

Activity 7: Infer from the Text 36

Activity 8: Predict from the Text... 45

Activity 9: Compare and Contrast 55

Activity 10: Analyze the Text by Examining the Use of Fact and Opinion..... 65

Activity 11: Explain How and Why the Author Uses Contents of a Text
to Support His/Her Purpose for Writing 79

Activity 12: Evaluate and Critique the Text for Organizational Structure 88

Activity 13: Evaluate and Critique the Text for Logic and Reasoning 97

Activity 14: Evaluate and Critique the Text 106

Activity 15: Summarize the Text 116

Activity 16: Identify Cause and Effect 132

Self-Scoring Chart.. 146

Introduction

What is *Read on Target*?

Read on Target is a book that has 16 reading maps to help you answer tough questions related to something that you have read. *Read on Target* gives students, like you, the tools you need to answer critical-thinking skill questions. Some of these skills include the ability to analyze story elements, to infer, to predict, and to compare and contrast. You will also need to know how to answer questions which ask you to analyze fact and opinion, explain how the author uses contents of the text to support his/her purpose of writing, critique, evaluate, summarize, and determine cause and effect. These are the important thinking skills that are found in this book. Many of these skills teach you how to break down information and to show the relationships in the text. The reading maps in *Read on Target* will guide you, step by step, through the process of answering these types of questions. Each reading map is designed to help you to reason and to understand what you read.

Why do you need *Read on Target*?

Sometimes when teachers or parents want to check your understanding of what you have read, they will want to know if you can reason and think critically about information. If you can answer these types of questions, you can show what you've learned. Sometimes it's hard to come up with the right answer when you don't know what the question is asking or how to answer the question. *Read on Target* will help you understand how to answer these questions. This book will also help you answer tough questions found on many of your tests. By using this book, you'll be more prepared to answer those questions you know your teachers or parents will ask.

Reading and understanding what you have read are two difficult tasks that you are expected to do for every subject. When you know how to read and how to understand the text, you can participate in class tasks better and answer those tough questions. You will continue to use these thinking skills as you enter the world of work.

How do you use *Read on Target*?

Read on Target will guide you through the process of answering critical-thinking questions correctly. *Read on Target* will tell you what to look for when you are reading. You will write your answers on the reading map and use your text as you need it. It can also be used to help you practice in your class and lets you see how someone else came up with a good answer. The next time you are asked to answer a critical-thinking question, you will be more prepared and better-equipped to provide a complete, well-thought out answer.

Activity 1

Analyze Aspects of the Text by Examining Characters

I read to figure out what the characters are like. I get to know them.

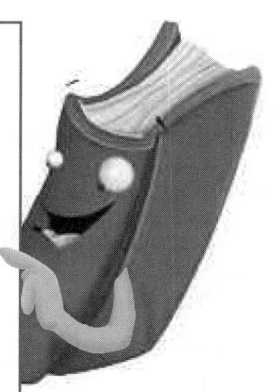

Step 1 Read the story "Friends."

Friends

It was a crisp fall day the first week in October. Olivia woke up, got dressed, brushed her hair, and came down to breakfast. Olivia always had a sunshiny smile that seemed to match her bright, yellow hair. She knew today was an extra special day because it was the day of the traveling art class. She was excited as she explained to her family that the art museum teachers were coming to her school. There would be drawing, painting, and lots of outside activities, too. Olivia smiled as she told her family about the art class where they would be able to draw and make art projects. She thought everyone in the class would just love this activity. Hurriedly, she finished her breakfast and went to school.

On the way to school, Olivia saw her friends Sally and Ann walking to school. Olivia told her friends she loved school, especially anything that had to do with drawing, and she had decided to bring her special pens and pink paper for drawing. She thought it would be a good idea to bring extra supplies so she could share with her friends.

Sally said, "I just love those pens and the pink paper. It will be fun to draw with them at school. That was really nice of you."

Olivia replied, "I brought 15 pens so all of my friends will have something to use during recess and art class." As the girls continued, Olivia saw more of her friends walking to school. She invited them to walk with Sally, Ann, and her. They talked excitedly about the upcoming art class.

Upon arriving at school, Olivia put her special pens and paper in the desk. She noticed her teacher had a sprained wrist. She felt very bad for her teacher, as she knew how painful a sprained wrist could be. Olivia drew a beautiful "Get Well Soon" card and quietly placed it on her teacher's desk. She hoped Mrs.

Activity 1  **Read on Target for Grade 6**

Smythe would feel better after reading the card. Of course, the teacher smiled when she saw the card. "What a nice surprise! Thank you so much, Olivia," said the teacher.

"You're welcome," Olivia replied shyly.

When Olivia returned to her seat, her pen fell out of her desk to the floor without her noticing. Ann picked it up and said, "Oh, this is my pen. I am so glad I found it." Ann mistakenly thought the pen was hers. Olivia did not say anything because she knew she had plenty more pens and was happy to let Ann keep that one. But during recess, Ann found Olivia and said, "I think this is your pen. I thought it was my pen, but after looking closer, I see it is yours. I am sorry."

Olivia replied, "Oh, thank you, but please just keep it as my gift to you." Ann was so happy to have this gift and thought Olivia was a good friend. She planned to share her art supplies with Olivia and her classmates during the art class.

The bell ending recess rang. Olivia and her friends went inside, as it was time for art class. "My favorite class!" exclaimed Olivia. She was even more excited when she saw how many different projects the children could choose to do. Olivia chose "Art and the Environment." Her teacher said they would plant acorns and try to grow an oak tree. Olivia smiled and said she would like that. Next, Olivia and her friends went outside and planted several acorns in the front schoolyard. They all hoped these would grow into big, beautiful oak trees someday. The children drew pictures of the small acorns and the trees that the acorns would someday grow to be. Olivia shared her pens and paper with her friends. They laughed and talked while they drew beautiful pictures. Olivia thought she was lucky to be able to share such a wonderful day with such good friends.

After school, Olivia and her friends talked about their day. They planned to check in the spring to see whether the acorns had grown into trees. Sure enough, that spring, Olivia came into the classroom and happily announced she had something to show everyone out in the schoolyard. The class was delighted to see some tiny sprouts coming up though the soil where they had planted the acorns. "These tiny sprouts should grow into big, beautiful trees," said Olivia. Her classmates brought out their art supplies and drew pictures of the sprouts. Everyone shared supplies.

Each year the baby oak trees grew larger and larger. Today, when Olivia brings her friends and family to the schoolyard, she tells them about when she and her friends planted the acorns. To this day, she has saved her art drawings of the acorns and the oak trees. She loves to look at them because they remind her of her friends and their fun activities in school.

Activity 1

Step 2 — Student Tips

To analyze a character you need to remember:
- A character can be a person, an animal, or an object.
- What the character is like, because this affects the story.
- The story could change if you change one part of a character.

Step 3

Complete the reading maps. Use the reading maps to help you think about the character.

Activity 1 *Read on Target* for Grade 6

Map 1.1

Analyze Aspects of the Text by Examining the Characters

I read to figure out what the characters are like. I get to know them.

Character's Name: _____

Describe the character.	What does the character look like?	How does the character act?	How does the character feel or think?	What does the character say?	What good or bad thing is the character doing?	How do others react to the character?
Write a sentence from the story that tells about the character.						
What does this tell you about the character?						

© 2006 ENGLEFIELD & ASSOCIATES, INC.

Activity 1 Read on Target for Grade 6

Map 1.2 Analyze Aspects of the Text by Examining the Characters

I read to figure out what the characters are like.
I get to know them.

Think about the sentences you wrote that describe the character.

How did the character affect the story?

_____

_____

_____

Give one quality you could change about the character.

_____

_____

_____

How would the story change if the character had this different quality?

_____

_____

_____

Activity 1 *Read on Target* for Grade 6

Step 4 — Read the following questions and write your answers.

1. What kind of person is Olivia? Give an example of something she said to support your answer.

   _____

   _____

   _____

2. Olivia has many friends. Based on what you read about her, what kinds of things does she do to make friends?

   _____

   _____

   _____

3. Olivia decides to quietly place her card on her teacher's desk. What does this tell you about Olivia?

   _____

   _____

   _____

4. Olivia doesn't say anything to Ann when Ann thinks the pen is hers. What does this tell you about Olivia?

   _____

   _____

   _____

Activity 2

Analyze Aspects of the Text by Examining Setting

I figure out how important the setting is and how the setting affects the characters and events that take place.

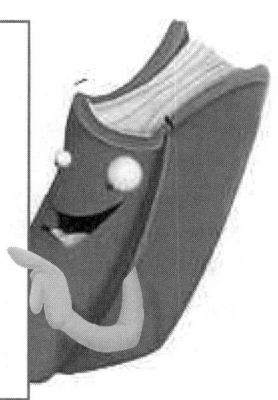

Step 1 Read the story "The Baseball Game."

The Baseball Game

It was a bright, sunny, summer day. Not a cloud was in the sky, and the wind was gently blowing the grass. Jason could hear the birds singing. It was a perfect day for a baseball game. Everyone in town came to watch the game. The fans sat on the bleachers wearing hats for shade. Jason was excited to be playing in the finals. He was especially glad it was not raining.

The vendors were out selling food and drinks. The hot dogs smelled good to Jason. Jason noticed they sold lots of soda pop, but people were not buying many hot dogs. Perhaps due to the heat, everyone was thirsty instead. The temperature was around 90 degrees. It was a hot day at the ballpark. The game had started at noon.

Now it was the last inning, and the score was tied. Jason stepped to the plate and waited for the first pitch. "Strike one!" shouted the umpire. Jason turned, looking at his dad and mom. He put the bat on his shoulder. Jason knew his parents had confidence in his ability to hit the ball. Jason adjusted his helmet. He was ready. Zoom! The ball whizzed by at the speed of light. Jason swung and missed as the second pitch went by. "Strike two!"

© 2006 Englefield & Associates, Inc.   COPYING IS PROHIBITED

Activity 2   *Read on Target* **for Grade 6**

"You can do it!" called Jason's dad from the stands. Jason wiped the sweat from his eyes.

"I know I can do it," he thought to himself. Sure enough, on the next pitch, Jason hit the ball to the edge of the park. He ran like the wind to first base, then off to second, and finally stopping at third. "Only one more base to go, and we win the game," thought Jason. "I just know I can do it." Jason's cousin, Michael, was up to bat. He swung the bat, and the ball flew off toward right field.

"Run, Jason, run!" yelled the coach. Jason started running, dirt and dust flying everywhere. He saw the ball fly through the air. The ball was screeching toward home plate. The catcher reached for the ball but dropped it. Jason could hardly breathe as he ran toward the plate. The catcher picked up the ball just as the Jason slid home. "Safe!" yelled the umpire.

"We won!" screamed Jason's coach; players and parents ran to the field to hug each other. Suddenly, a rain cloud came out of nowhere, pouring down on the players and fans. It rained buckets and buckets. The players' dusty uniforms became coated in mud. "The only good thing about this rain," said Jason, "is that it cooled us off. I'm sure glad we didn't have to cancel the game."

The players ran out onto the field to pick up their equipment. The uniforms had become a slimy brownish-black color. The field had become a slippery, muddy mess. The players slipped and slid across the field as they picked up their equipment. "What a mess!" declared Jason.

The clouds blew away as quickly as they had come, and the rain stopped as suddenly as it had started. "Now we are all ready to eat hot dogs," cried the players. The vendors happily sold all of the food. Everyone was ready to go home.

"What a great game!" said Jason.

"I agree," said his cousin Michael. They looked at the mud on each other and laughed.

"I bet my mother will have lots of laundry to do when we get home," said Jason.

Activity 2   *Read on Target* **for Grade 6**

Step 2: Student Tips

To analyze the setting, you need to remember:

- What the setting looks like. Tell where the story takes place, tell when the story takes place, and tell what you hear, feel, and smell.

- The setting affects the story. If the setting is a sunny day, you might feel warm and happy. If the setting is a dark night, you might feel scared.

- The story could change if you change one part of the setting.

Step 3: Complete the reading maps. Use the reading maps to help you think about the setting.

Activity 2　　　　　　　　　　　　　　　　Read on Target for Grade 6

Map 2.1   Analyze Aspects of the Text by Examining Setting

I figure out how important the setting is and how the setting influences the characters and events that take place.

Describe the setting.	
	Write words or sentences from the text that tell about the setting.
Tell where the story takes place.	
Tell when the story takes place.	
Tell what you hear in the setting.	
Tell what you feel in the setting.	
Tell what you smell in the setting.	
Tell what you see in the setting.	

10　　　　COPYING IS PROHIBITED　　　　© 2006 Englefield & Associates, Inc.

Activity 2   Read on Target for Grade 6

Map 2.2   Analyze Aspects of the Text by Examining Setting

I figure out how important the setting is and how the setting influences the characters and events that take place.

Think about the setting.

How does the setting affect the characters?

_____
_____

How does the setting affect the events of the story?

_____
_____

Now, change the setting.

Change what the setting looks like to **a sunny day that never rains**. Tell how the story would be different.

_____
_____
_____

Change where the setting is (where the story takes place) to **inside a gym on Monday at 9:00 a.m.** Tell how the story would be different.

_____
_____
_____

Activity 2   Read on Target for Grade 6

Step 4 — Read the following questions and write your answers.

1. Game day was described as bright, sunny, and hot. How did the setting affect the vendor's ability to sell hot dogs?

   _____

   _____

   _____

2. How would the events in the story change if it rained at the beginning of the story?

   _____

   _____

   _____

3. How would the story change if it remained a hot, sunny day throughout the story?

   _____

   _____

   _____

4. What aspects of the setting could be different without changing the events in the story?

   _____

   _____

   _____

Activity 3

Analyze Aspects of the Text by Examining Plot
I read to figure out the chain of events; what will happen next.

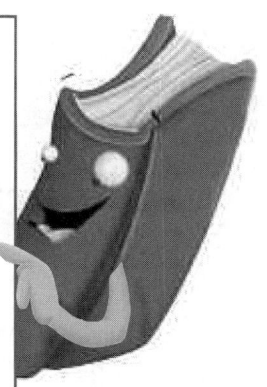

Step 1 Read the story "A Hike in the Woods."

A Hike in the Woods

I can still remember the day we went hiking in the woods. It was in the late autumn. The sun was a bright lemon yellow, and the sky was as blue as the ocean. It was a good day to be outside. My cousins, Samantha, Joey, Michael, and Hannah, and I were visiting our aunt and uncle. They live on a farm near the wooded mountains. We decided it would be a great idea to hike up to the very top of the mountain closest to their farm.

First, we had to gather our hiking gear. We would need hiking shoes, warm hats, food, water, and most importantly, a compass. It took most of the morning to find everything we needed, but eventually we found everything we thought was important for our hike. I could not believe how much hiking gear we needed!

Next, we said goodbye to our aunt and uncle as we went off to hike up the mountain. The ground around the farm was covered with a blanket of yellow asters. The gentle breeze made them move as if they were dancing in the fields. Bluebirds and robins poked their sharp beaks into the ground searching for worms. The cows chewed lazily on the tall grass as we passed by.

As we continued up the mountain, we noticed the trees were taller and grew closer together than they had at the altitude of the farm. It was just like looking at a wall of wood. I thought it would be a great place to have a tree house. As we climbed higher and higher, it became colder and colder. I even saw snow on the ground. It was time to stop, to eat, and to rest. We decided to put on our hats. I certainly was glad we packed them. We then ate our food, which consisted of sandwiches, chips, cookies, and drinks. It tasted delicious, and we ate every bite. After eating and resting, we continued our trip. It was a perfect place to hike.

© 2006 Englefield & Associates, Inc.   COPYING IS PROHIBITED

At last, we reached the top. "Oh," said my cousins, "the view is incredible!" We could see the town far below. Our aunt and uncle's bright yellow house and big red barn stood out against the green hills below. We could also see small rivers and a lake. The farmland down below looked like a green patchwork quilt. It was exciting for us to discover all the beautiful things to see when hiking. We lingered there enjoying all the beauty.

As we started down the mountain, my cousins and I realized the sun was sinking lower, and we were lost! We no longer could see the town or our aunt and uncle's house. The trees seemed to close up around us. We were scared! All I could think about was getting home. "Oh no!" I said. My only thought was my fear of not being able to descend the mountain before the weather turned to snow. If snow came, the footholds on the trail would be as slippery as glass. "Let's get going!" I cried. I had no idea where I was going. Suddenly, I remembered that I brought the compass. "Hooray!" I cried, "I think we are going to find our way home."

Finally, we made it home to the farm. A chilly breeze had started to blow, pelting sharp rain on us, and we could see snow swirling at the top of the mountain. We were glad to be inside in a warm house. Our aunt and uncle were glad that we packed hiking supplies, especially the compass. Those supplies helped make the hike a success. What an adventure! But I was relieved to be home safe and sound.

Activity 3 *Read on Target* for Grade 6

Step 2 — Student Tips

To analyze the plot, you need to remember:

- The plot is the chain of events in the story. The plot has a beginning, a middle, and an ending. The plot has a problem and a solution.
- The plot affects the characters and events.
- When the plot changes, the story changes. What happens to the plot if you change the order of an event? What happens to the plot if you take out an event? What happens to the plot if you change a character's actions?

Step 3 — Complete the reading maps. Use the reading maps to help you think about the plot.

Activity 3
Read on Target for Grade 6

Map 3.1

Analyze Aspects of the Text by Examining Plot
I read to figure out the chain of events; what will happen next.

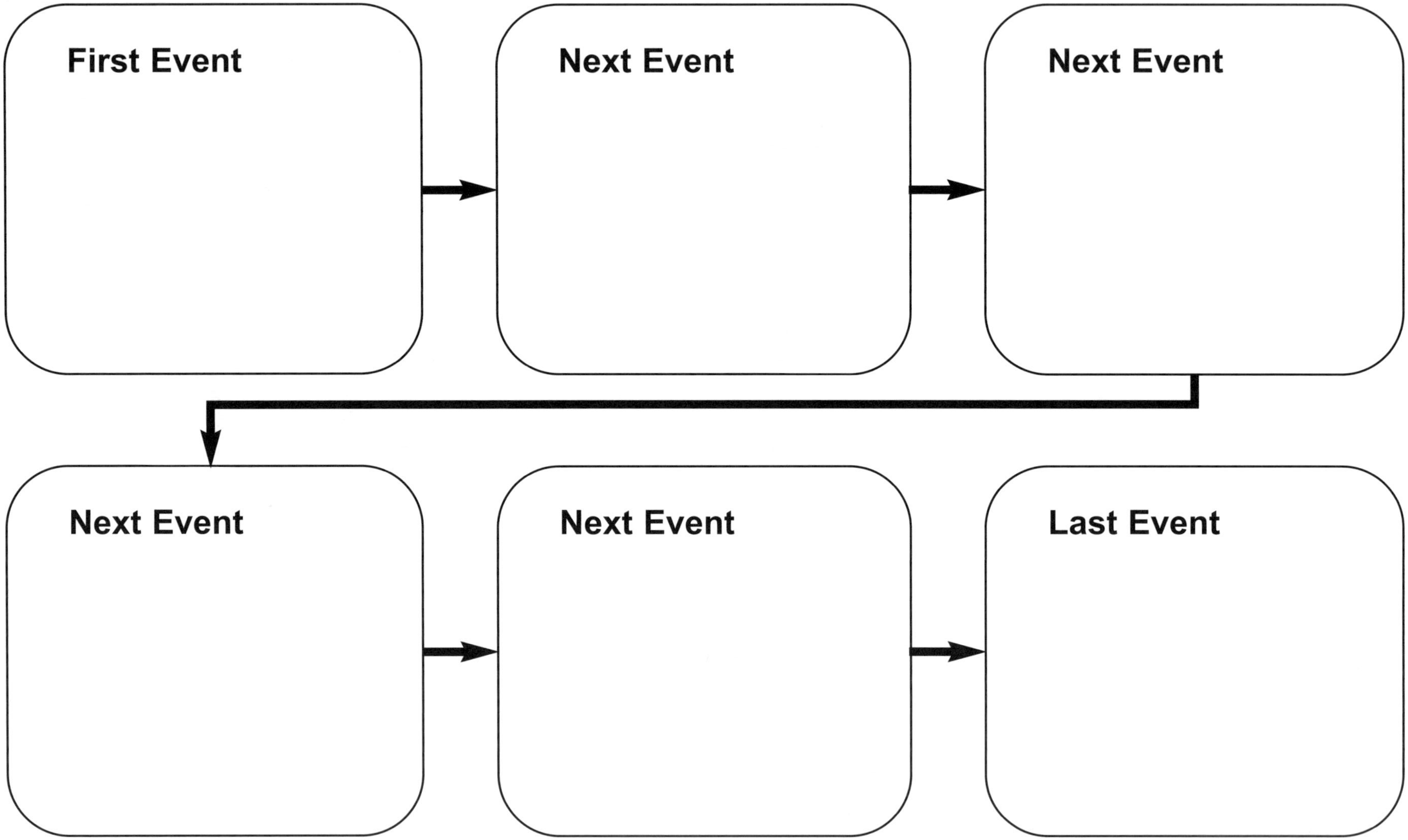

- First Event → Next Event → Next Event → Next Event
- Next Event → Next Event → Last Event

Activity 3   Read on Target for Grade 6

Map 3.2   Analyze Aspects of the Text
by Examining Plot
I read to figure out the chain of events;
what will happen next.

Change the Plot.

Choose an event to happen earlier or later. Write the event you choose.
_____

How might the story be different if one of the events happened earlier or later?
_____
_____
_____

Take an event out of the story. Write the event you choose.
_____

How might the story be different if one of the events is left out of the story?
_____
_____
_____

What would happen if the characters' actions were different?
_____
_____
_____

Activity 3   **Read on Target** for Grade 6

Step 4
Read the following questions and write your answers.

1. Why did the cousins pack hiking gear prior to starting out on their hike?

   _____
   _____
   _____

2. What could have happened if the cousins had forgotten to pack food?

   _____
   _____
   _____

3. How do the cousins find their way home?

   _____
   _____
   _____

4. How would the story be different if a sudden snowstorm occurred while the cousins were at the top of the mountain?

   _____
   _____
   _____

Activity 4

Analyze Aspects of the Text by Examining Problem/Solution

I read to figure out the problem and how it is solved.

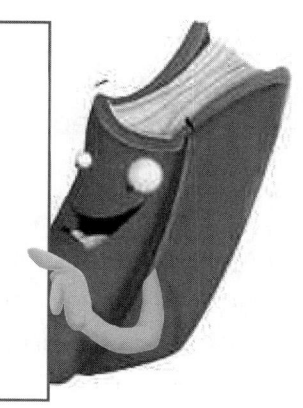

Step 1 Read the story "One School Morning."

One School Morning

It was a gloomy, gusty, gray, and rainy morning. The wind whipped around the trees and sounded like a train whistle. It was the kind of day for sleeping late, and Pam's warm covers offered her a cozy nest to stay in all day long.

Unfortunately, it was a school day, and Pam was sound asleep in her bed. The alarm clock sat silently on the night stand beside her bed. The noise of the wind woke Pam. "Oh no!" said Pam as she rubbed the sleep from her eyes. "I am going to be late to school!" She checked her alarm clock to find out why it had not done its job. She knew she had set it the night before. As she pressed the button to see the time the alarm was set for, she discovered she was right—she had set her alarm the night before . . . for 7:15 p.m.! She ran to the window just in time to see the back of the school bus as it pulled away from her house.

Pam rushed around the house. She needed to find her clothes and school supplies. She thought to herself, "I should have laid out these clothes last night. What am I going to do?" Her sock drawer was a mess, but she finally managed to find two matching socks. She saw one shoe under her bed, but it took her a few moments to find its

© 2006 Englefield & Associates, Inc.   COPYING IS PROHIBITED   19

Activity 4   **Read on Target for Grade 6**

match, which had somehow ended up downstairs behind the couch. "Why me?" Pam moaned. "Of all mornings, why does everything have to be so difficult **this** morning!"

"Now, I am almost ready to go. All I need to do is make my lunch," said Pam. No time for anything fancy this morning. She quickly grabbed the jars of peanut butter and jelly from the refrigerator. Her fingers flew as she spread first peanut butter and then jelly on two pieces of white bread. She returned the jars to the fridge and was going to rinse off the knife when it suddenly slipped from her hand, smearing grape jelly down the front of her favorite T-shirt. "No time to worry about it now," Pam thought to herself as she continued to pack her lunch. An apple, a small bag of chips, and a juice box made her lunch complete. She grabbed her backpack and ran out the door with her lunch in hand.

As she ran off the front porch, she tripped on a branch that had fallen to the ground during the storm the night before. She fell right into a fresh puddle of mud. To make matters worse, she had landed on her lunch. The bag began to turn a strange purple color. She peeked inside to discover not only had she smashed her sandwich, but her juice box had exploded, and the jelly and juice were combining to form a sickening purple soup. What a mess! Pam had no choice but to go back in the house and start all over again! Now, she was really late.

As she entered the school building, the principal asked, "Why are you late?" Pam wished she had not overslept. "This is the fourth time this school year that you have been late," said the principal.

"I know," said Pam. She continued, "I just woke up late again."

"I want you to think how you can solve this problem," said the principal. Pam agreed to think about her problem.

As she went to class, she thought about several ways to solve her problem. One way could be to ask her parents to call and excuse her. Another way could be to sneak into school. She did not think these would be good solutions. Pam asked her friends what they would do. Her friends said they could stop by her house in the morning to make sure she was awake. They thought she might want to ask her parents to help her too. Most importantly, they said it was up to Pam to make sure she set her clock correctly!

When Pam got home from school that day, she decided to have a fresh start. She threw out her old alarm clock, which had been giving her problems, and asked her parents to buy her a new one. Each night, she carefully set the alarm to wake her up on time. Her family and friends also helped to make sure she was getting up on time. Sure enough, the new plan worked, and she was never late to school again.

Activity 4 Read on Target for Grade 6

Step 2 — Student Tips

To analyze the problem/solution, you need to remember:

- A problem from the story can be something the character wants to change or something the character wants to do.
- A solution from the story can be an action taken to solve the problem, or it can be a decision.
- The problem and solution help you understand the plot.
- If you change the problem, think about how the events from the story or the solution could change.

Step 3 — Complete the reading maps. Use the reading maps to help you think about the problem and solution.

Activity 4   *Read on Target* **for Grade 6**

Map 4.1 — Analyze Aspects of the Text by Examining Problem/Solution

I read to figure out the problem and how it is solved.

Read the definition of a problem and a solution.

The **problem** can be:	The **solution** can be:
• A situation that the character wants to change. • Something the character wants to do or to find out.	• An action that helps the character understand how the problem is solved. • A decision that helps the character understand how the problem is solved.

What is the problem? _____

_____

_____

What events help solve the problem?

    Event 1. _____

    Event 2. _____

    Event 3. _____

What is the solution? _____

_____

_____

Activity 4   Read on Target for Grade 6

Map 4.2   Analyze Aspects of the Text by
Examining Problem/Solution
I read to figure out the problem and how it is solved.

Change the problem by making up a different problem.

Write your made-up problem on these lines. _____
_____
_____

How would the events be different?

    Event 1. _____
                 _____

    Event 2. _____
                 _____

    Event 3. _____
                 _____

How would the solution be different?
_____
_____
_____
_____

Activity 4 *Read on Target* **for Grade 6**

Step 4
Read the following questions and write your answers.

1. What is Pam's problem?

2. Pam thought about several solutions as a way to solve her problem. List the solutions that she considered.

3. What did Pam's friends suggest as a way to solve Pam's problem?

4. If the problem changed to become Pam forgetting her homework, how would the events be different?

Activity 5

Analyze Aspects of the Text by Examining Point of View

I figure out the author's choice of speaker. I also think why the author chose to write from this point of view and how the story would be different if the story were told from another point of view.

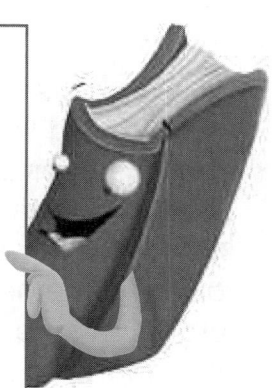

Step 1 Read the story "The Cave."

The Cave

Jacob and his friends, Carlos and Peter, had a great interest in studying plants, rocks, and small animals that lived in the nearby mountains. They were also very interested in the terrain and history of the surrounding area. Jacob became very excited one day after reading about paintings found in a nearby cave. "Look at the article in this newspaper. There are paintings that must have been done by early mankind," said Peter, showing the article to his friends.

Carlos replied, "I think the paintings are called hieroglyphics."

"Let's see if we can find the cave," said Peter. Carlos was just a little afraid he might get lost. He did not want his friends to know how he felt because he did not want to be teased. Jacob was a little anxious and would rather have stayed behind. He didn't want to be made fun of either. As a result, he agreed to go in search of the cave.

"Let's go!" they cried. The boys began searching for the cave. Just then, at the foot of a bluff, they saw the cave.

"Here it is!" shouted Peter. The boys scrambled up to the cave.

Jacob thought to himself, "We had better make sure we don't lose our way. I have a string in my pocket that we can use to find our way back in case we get lost in the cave."

Entering the dark gloomy cave, they could see several passages with long dark walkways. "If we find more of the drawings, we will be famous," said Jacob.

"No kidding?" questioned Peter. "Well," he thought, "if I am going to be famous, then I better keep moving in this cave." "Come along," he said aloud, "let's keep going."

© 2006 Englefield & Associates, Inc.   COPYING IS PROHIBITED   25

The boys continued to wander through the intricate maze of passages. They were having little luck in their search. Just then, Carlos noticed a small opening near the floor of the passage they were in. The boys were hesitant to crawl through the narrow opening, but they were not about to give up. On hands and knees, they crawled through the ever-narrowing passageway. They continued on for what seemed like hundreds of yards. Finally, the passage opened up into a large, cavernous room. The three boys emerged and shined their flashlights around the room. On the walls, they saw primitive drawings and designs of people and animals. They stood in awe as they gazed at the ancient gallery.

Suddenly, they heard a loud clap of thunder. Peter looked up with a troubled frown. "I think we better look at the weather. These drawings will be here later." Carlos was wondering how in the world they would find their way out of the cave.

Peter was beginning to get scared. He was wishing he had not suggested to his friends that they search for the cave. Jacob thought, "The string will surely save the day. I know just how to get out of here." Jacob noticed that his friends were quiet. He said, "What's wrong?"

His friends replied, "We are lost in this cave!" They just wanted to go home before the storm got any worse.

Jacob grinned at them and pulled out the string. "This is tied to a tree at the front of the cave. All we need to do is just follow the string."

Carlos whooped, "You saved the day!" Jacob was right. The boys followed the trail of string out of the cave. They made it home before the rain started. All the boys were glad Jacob remembered to use the string. He had indeed saved the day!

Activity 5   *Read on Target* **for Grade 6**

Step 2 — Student Tips

- Make sure you know the definitions and key words of each point of view. You will find the definitions in the Reading Map.

- Think about the reason the author wrote from this point of view.

- Did the author write to let you know what was in the mind of several selected characters only, or did the author let you know what every character was thinking? Perhaps the author told the story to allow you to step into the shoes of the main character.

- Consider how changing the point of view will affect how you feel or think about what you have read. This will give you a clue as to why the author wrote from that point of view.

Step 3 — Complete the reading maps. Use the reading maps to help you think about the author's point of view.

Activity 5   *Read on Target for Grade 6*

Map 5.1 — Analyze Aspects of the Text by Examining Point of View

I figure out the author's choice of speaker. I also think about why the author chose to write from this point of view and how the story would be different if the story were told from another point of view.

Point of View	Definition	Key Word Pronouns: They tell the author's choice of speaker.
First-Person	I am in the story. I tell the story.	I, me, my, we, us, our
Third-Person	Someone outside of the story tells the story from what he/she knows.	he, she, they, them
Omniscient (All-Knowing)	Someone outside of the story tells the story but knows what everyone sees, feels, and thinks.	he, she, they, them

	Write one or more sentences from the story that helped you figure out the author's point of view.
What is the Point of View? (circle who tells the story) 1. First-Person 2. Third-Person 3. Omniscient (All-Knowing)	

28   COPYING IS PROHIBITED   © 2006 Englefield & Associates, Inc.

Activity 5   ***Read on Target* for Grade 6**

Map 5.2   **Analyze Aspects of the Text by Examining Point of View**

I figure out the author's choice of speaker. I also think about why the author chose to write from this point of view and how the story would be different if the story were told from another point of view.

Why did the author write from this point of view?

_____
_____
_____
_____
_____

Change the point of view to first-person. How is the story different?

_____
_____
_____
_____
_____

Activity 5   **Read on Target** for Grade 6

Step 4
Read the following questions and write your answers.

1. How did you figure out the point of view of this story?

2. At first, only Jacob knew he had used a string to help him find the way out of the cave. How did you feel knowing that Carlos and Peter were worried about becoming lost in the cave?

3. How might the story be different if both Carlos and Jacob knew that Peter was afraid he might get lost going to the cave?

4. What point of view would an author most likely use if he or she wrote this story as an autobiography?

Activity 6

Analyze Aspects of the Text by Examining Theme

I figure out the overall message the author is telling me.

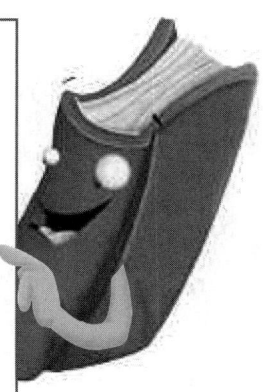

Step 1 Read the story "The Rodeo Ride."

The Rodeo Ride

In my backyard, you can see a lot of animals running around, the funniest of which are a squirrel and a rabbit. I call the squirrel Buster and consider him to be a part of the family, and our family rabbit is named Thumper.

Usually, Buster the squirrel scampers along the leafy branches of the trees. He peers out from his holes in the back of the lawn. Then, he jumps from tree to tree, collecting nuts and berries. Buster is a very busy squirrel.

Our rabbit, Thumper, is black and white. He weighs about 10 pounds. Thumper is soft, furry, and hops around the yard very fast. He nibbles on grass and plants in the yard and runs out of sight when he senses danger.

Our backyard can be full of fun and adventure for the animals. Sometimes, Thumper the rabbit likes to take Buster's food. Because Thumper can hop very fast, Buster has trouble catching him. This seems to make Buster mad enough that he sometimes sits on a tree limb, chattering angrily at Thumper from a distance.

Just yesterday, Mr. Nathan put out the sunflower seeds and nuts for Buster to eat. He put the food bowl under a crabapple tree. Thumper was quietly watching the food bowl. He decided to investigate the food bowl, but he did not see Buster in the tree above, so he hopped right up to the food bowl. Buster looked down at Thumper. He seemed so angry that this time, he didn't even chatter at Thumper. I'll bet Buster was thinking about how to teach Thumper a lesson for stealing his food. Buster appeared angrier every minute because Thumper continued to eat the food. He was going to finish all of it if nothing stopped him. Buster began to chatter angrily. Thumper didn't seem to listen, he just nibbled away at the food in the bowl.

Activity 6   ***Read on Target* for Grade 6**

    Suddenly, Buster jumped right out of the tree. That squirrel landed right on the back of the black and white ten-pound rabbit. Unbelievably, Thumper had a squirrel right on his back! It looked like a cowboy riding a bronco horse in a rodeo. Buster's little squirrel legs held on tight. That angry squirrel fussed with Thumper, while all the time Thumper was bucking, hopping, and running all around the yard. Everyone laughed. It was the funniest sight we had ever seen.

    Soon enough, Thumper stopped bucking and Buster jumped off. The rodeo ride was over! Thumper quickly hopped away from Buster's food bowl, all the while seeming confused about what had just happened. From that day on, Thumper never ate Buster's food, and Buster has never ridden on top of Thumper again. It looks like Thumper has learned his lesson.

Activity 6 Read on Target for Grade 6

Step 2 — Student Tips

To analyze theme, you need to remember:

- There are important ideas from the story. Look for words that tell about the story. Look for repeated words.

- The character might learn lessons. Think about how the character feels and thinks. Think about what happened to the character.

- There is an overall message of the story.

Step 3 — Complete the reading map. Use the reading map to help you think about the theme.

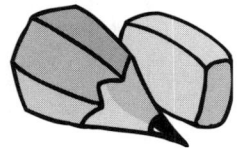

Activity 6   Read on Target for Grade 6

Map 6   Analyze Aspects of the Text by
                                Examining Theme
             I figure out the overall message that the author is telling me.

Name some of the ideas that you learned from the story.

_____
_____
_____
_____
_____

What lessons did the character or characters learn?

_____
_____
_____

Write a sentence telling what you think the theme of the story is.

_____
_____
_____

Activity 6

Step 4 Read the following questions and write your answers.

1. What did Thumper do with Buster's food?

   _____
   _____
   _____

2. How did Buster react to Thumper eating his food?

   _____
   _____
   _____

3. What lesson did Thumper learn?

   _____
   _____
   _____

4. What is the theme of the story?

   _____
   _____
   _____

Activity 7a

Infer from the Text

I read clues and use what I know to figure out what is happening in the story.

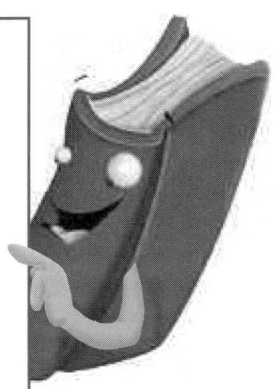

Step 1 Read the story "The Best Day."

The Best Day

It was cold, and the yard was covered in white. The ground looked as smooth as frosting with its tiny swirls and peaks. It was so deep that people were having difficulty walking outside. Seth peeked out from his blanket. The warmth was in sharp contrast to the frost that edged the windows, leaving only a limited view of the outside world. Marcus looked at his alarm clock and wondered why it had not rung. "Oh, yes! It is Saturday, no school today!" he cried as he leaped out of his bed.

Peering out a clear spot the frosty window, Marcus noticed his neighbor was trying to walk toward the mailbox. It was so deep, his neighbor, Mr. Ambrosia, looked like he was wading through a mound of sticky cotton. Marcus decided to shovel the walkway. He put on his coat and hurried outside.

After shoveling the walk, Marcus came inside. He noticed his new sled in the hall. Mom and Dad had given Marcus and Seth a matching pair for their birthday a few days ago. "Make sure you put these on so your heads will stay warm," said Mom, handing something to each boy as he walked through the front door. The boys were off to the city park. They had a great time racing their new sleds down the hill. The cold wind numbed their faces as they slid swiftly through the snow. The boys were glad that Mom reminded them to wear their winter gear. They remained comfortable the whole time they were sledding.

Upon returning home, they smelled something sweet. It reminded the boys of cinnamon sticks and sugar. Mom had been baking all afternoon. They saw some round, soft circles on the cooling rack. Best of all, some were left on a plate for the boys. Marcus and Seth rushed to the table and ate all of them quickly. "This is great!" they exclaimed. "What a super way to end the day!" The boys decided today was the best day yet.

Activity 7a Read on Target for Grade 6

Step 2 — Student Tips

To infer from the story, you need to remember:

- There are clues in the story. Clues are hints the author gives you about the story. Draw a line under each clue, or use your finger to point to the clue.

- What you know will help you figure out the story. Think about what is going on in the story. Have you done it before? Do you know about it?

- Clues, experiences, and knowledge are put together.

- Using clues from the the story and what you know will help you figure out what is happening in the story. (This is called an **inference**.)

Step 3 — Complete the reading map. Use the reading map to help you think about inferring.

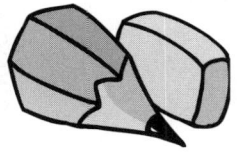

Activity 7a — *Read on Target for Grade 6*

Map 7a

Infer from the Text

I read clues and use my knowledge to figure out what is happening in the story.

My Clues +

Find the clues in each sentence. Write your clues in the boxes below.

- Clues about what was on the ground.
- Clues to tell you what the boys put on to keep them warm.
- Clues about what the boys ate.

My Experiences =

Think about your experiences and knowledge of a similar thing. Write your information in the boxes below.

- Your experiences and knowledge of a similar thing.
- Your experiences and knowledge of a similar thing.
- Your experiences and knowledge of a similar thing.

My Inference

Put the clues and experience/knowledge together to make a guess about what is happening in the story.

- What was on the ground?
- What did the boys put on their heads.
- What did the boys eat?

38 — COPYING IS PROHIBITED — © 2006 ENGLEFIELD & ASSOCIATES, INC.

Activity 7a *Read on Target* for Grade 6

Step 4
Read the following questions and write your answers.

1. What clues told you the neighbor was walking in snow?

   _____
   _____
   _____

2. What clues tell you the boys are twins?

   _____
   _____
   _____

3. What did the boys put on their heads? How do you know?

   _____
   _____
   _____

4. What did the boys eat when they returned home from sledding?

   _____
   _____
   _____

Activity 7b

Infer from the Text
I read clues and use what I know to figure out what is happening in the story.

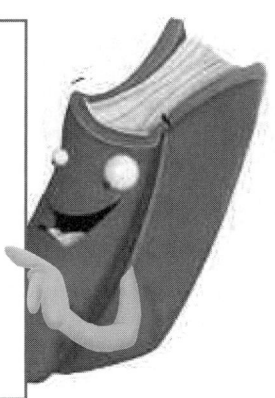

Step 1 Read the story "Away From Home."

Away From Home

Our car drove down the winding lane, through the woods, past the swimming pool, and finally around the lake. We passed many groups of cabins, soccer and baseball fields, and even a giant tree swing. After we finally came to a stop, I opened the car door and slowly picked up my sleeping bag and suitcase. "Bye Mom," I said with a frown. This was my first time away from home. Even worse, I had to leave my most treasured possession behind: my bike!

"Have a wonderful time, and don't forget to write," said Mom. I watched as the car slowly crept back down the lane. Unfamiliar kids were everywhere, hurrying and laughing with one another, carrying their bags and suitcases into the different cabins that surrounded the area. My legs felt like wood as I made my way slowly to Cabin 4, a building I would have to call home for the next two weeks whether I liked it or not.

My sleeping bag felt heavy in my arms. I knew I was not supposed to cry, but I just couldn't help it. I had never been away from home. This was my first time at this place. I did not know if I could get used to the idea of spending two whole weeks away from home, away from my bike, and with so many strangers!

As I walked shaking like a leaf through the cabin door, two people looked at me. They sat quietly and looked just the way I felt. We all turned around as we saw a woman walk through the door and into our cabin. "This must be our cabin leader," I thought to myself.

"Hi, I am Juanita," said the woman as she approached the three of us. "You must be Jane, Carol, and Marci," she added. "It is time to check out the activities. Follow me." She smiled warmly.

As we strolled around, Juanita showed us all of the highlights. First, she showed us all the different sports fields. There were fields for baseball, soccer, and football as well as a big open area for whatever game we could think of to amuse ourselves. She told us any equipment we needed was kept in the building where we would be eating our meals. She also pointed out many different trails which could be used for hiking or any other purpose. She then took us by the lake and showed us the area that had been roped off for swimming. It even had a rope swing to jump off the dock! Next to the lake was a shed. As we approached it, Juanita explained to us that some equipment, such as canoes for the lake, were too big to be kept anywhere else, so a shed was built for them. As Juanita opened the shed to display its contents, my heart skipped a beat as some of the equipment caught my eye. They were shiny, new, and looked to be just the right size. I started to smile, as did my two cabin mates.

Then we were off down the dirt trails Juanita had shown us earlier! I was on the red and gold racer with red handlebars. I quickly turned out of sight. As we came around the bend, Juanita let out a cry and cheered us on. Carol pulled in front of us and raced to the front of the line. Soon, Marci pulled up to the lead. We had a great time no matter who was in front.

We returned to the cabin and unpacked our bags. I heard a friendly voice in the bunk next to mine ask, "Hi, Jane, want to ride later?" It was Carol.

Smiling, I said, "I would love to."

Activity 7b   *Read on Target* for Grade 6

Step 2 — Student Tips

To infer from the story, you need to remember:

- There are clues in the story. Clues are hints the author gives you about the story. Draw a line under each clue, or use your finger to point to the clue.

- What you know will help you figure out the story. Think about what is going on in the story. Have you done it before? Do you know about it?

- Clues, experiences, and knowledge are put together.

- Using clues from the the story and what you know will help you figure out what is happening in the story. (This is called an **inference**.)

Step 3

Complete the reading map. Use the reading map to help you think about inferring.

Activity 7b  *Read on Target* for Grade 6

Infer from the Text

I read clues and use my knowledge to figure out what is happening in the story.

Map 7b

My Clues +

Find the clues in each sentence. Write your clues in the boxes below.

My Experiences =

Think about your experiences and knowledge of a similar thing. Write your information in the boxes below.

My Inference

Put the clues and experience/knowledge together to make a guess about what is happening in the story.

Clues to tell you where Jane is. → Your experiences and knowledge of a similar thing. → Where is Jane?

Clues to tell you what she rode. → Your experiences and knowledge of a similar thing. → What did she ride?

Clues to tell you what Jane's final attitude is about camp. → Your experiences and knowledge of a similar thing. → Is Jane enjoying camp?

© 2006 Englefield & Associates, Inc.   COPYING IS PROHIBITED

Activity 7b   **Read on Target** for Grade 6

Step 4 — Read the following questions and write your answers.

1. Where is Jane? What clues told you where Jane is?

   _____
   _____
   _____

2. What is Jane riding on the trail? What clues helped you figure it out?

   _____
   _____
   _____

3. How did you figure out if Jane is enjoying camp?

   _____
   _____
   _____

4. What is your experience or knowledge that helped you figure out what Jane rode?

   _____
   _____
   _____

Activity 8a

Predict from the Text

I read clues and use my knowledge to figure out what will happen in the future.

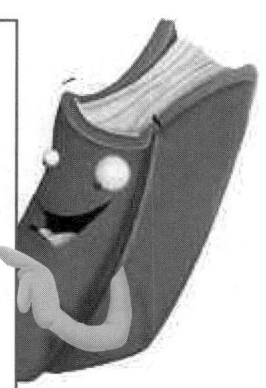

Step 1   Read the passage "The Bike Trail."

The Bike Trail

Keesha had been thinking about becoming a scientist when she is older. Keesha had learned in science class that something will stay in motion until an opposing force causes it to stop. She thought about making observations and making predictions based upon her observations. She also thought her observations would help her figure out what might happen in the future when a similar thing occurs. She decided to practice collecting data based on her observations. One day after school, she sat in the cool shade under a tree while watching kids on bikes, skateboards, and inline skates. Keesha saw a bike rider run into a pothole. He came to a sudden stop. His helmet fell forward. Based on her observations and knowledge, Keesha wrote some prediction questions.

First Prediction Question: A girl with a long ponytail is riding her bike. The ponytail is pointing out straight behind her back as she rides. The bike suddenly stops. What happens to her ponytail?

© 2006 Englefield & Associates, Inc.   COPYING IS PROHIBITED

Activity 8a   *Read on Target* **for Grade 6**

Second Prediction Question: A skateboarder is coming down the hill at a fast speed. Her skateboard runs off the bike trail and hits a wall of stone. What happens to the skateboard?

Third Prediction Question: A boy on in-line skates is on the bike path. He is coming down the hill. He applies his brakes in a sudden motion. What happens to the person on in-line skates?

Keesha recorded her observations on a prediction chart and wondered what would happen in the future if someone ran into a pothole that was on the bike path. She thought a good scientist would use observations as one way to think about what might happen in the future. Keesha planned to continue to use observation as a method of scientific investigation.

Activity 8a Read on Target for Grade 6

Step 2 — Student Tips

To predict from the text, you need to remember:

- There are clues in the story. Clues are hints the author gives you about the story. Draw a line under each clue, or use your finger to point to the clue.

- What you know will help you make a guess about what will happen next in the story. Think about what is going on in the story. Have you done it before? Do you know about it?

- Clues, experiences, and knowledge are put together.

- Using clues from the story and what you know will help you figure out what will happen next. (This is called a **prediction**.)

Step 3 — Complete the reading map. Use the reading map to help you think about predicting.

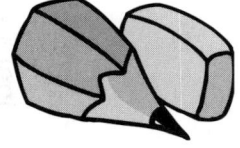

Activity 8a *Read on Target* for Grade 6

Map 8a

Infer from the Text

I read clues and use my knowledge to figure out what is happening in the story.

My Clues + **My Experiences** = **My Prediction**

Find clues in each sentence or paragraph that would help you answer the questions from the passage.

Think about your experiences and knowledge of a similar thing. Write your information in the boxes below.

Put the clues and experience/knowledge together to make a guess about what is happening in the story.

My Clues	My Experiences	My Prediction
Clues about what happens to the ponytail.	Your experiences and knowledge of a similar thing.	What will happen to the ponytail?
Clues about the skateboard and the rider.	Your experiences and knowledge of a similar thing.	What do you think will happen to the skateboard and the rider?
Clues about the in-line skater.	Your experiences and knowledge of a similar thing.	What do you think will happen to the person on the in-line skates?

48   COPYING IS PROHIBITED   © 2006 Englefield & Associates, Inc.

Activity 8a Read on Target for Grade 6

Step 4
Read the following questions and write your answers.

1. What do you think will happen to the skateboard and the rider?

   _____

   _____

   _____

2. How did you figure out the answer to question 1?

   _____

   _____

   _____

3. What do you think will happen to the person on the in-line skates?

   _____

   _____

   _____

4. What clues from the passage helped you figure out what happens to the girl's ponytail after the bike suddenly stops?

   _____

   _____

   _____

Activity 8b

Predict from the Text
I read clues and use my knowledge to figure out what will happen in the future.

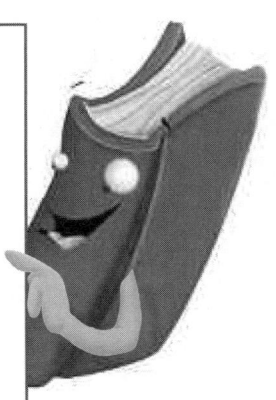

Step 1   Read the information in "A Day at the Beach."

A Day at the Beach

On Friday, Jordan and her brother, Michael, pack their bags. They are ready to go to Grandmother and Grandfather's beach house for a week-long summer vacation. Both children are excited to see the crystal blue water and golden sand. They always get up early and go to bed late because there are so many activities to do at the beach. They enjoy fishing, making sandcastles, and swimming in the ocean.

Each of them has a new activity to try on this vacation. Michael's new activity is surfing. Michael wants to learn how to surf on his new, bright, shiny board. He loves the thought of surfing when the wave action is fast and furious. He knows the best time to surf is at high tide.

Jordan would likes to collect unusual seashells. She has collected seashells before, but this year, she hopes to find many different kinds of shells on the beach.

Activity 8b   Read on Target for Grade 6

Jordan found an old chart in the living room. It listed the schedule of the tides. The schedule was for last week, the week before they arrived at the beach. They think there is enough information in the chart that will give clues to tell them when the tides will be low and high during the week of their vacation. Low tide is when the water recedes and more land is exposed, and the water is calmer at low tide. High tide is when the water reaches its highest point and covers the most land. At high tide, the big waves crash one after another. Here is what part of the tide chart looked like.

	Monday	Tuesday	Wednesday	Thursday	Friday
Low Tide	5:04 a.m.	5:09 a.m.	5:15 a.m.	5:22 a.m.	5:30 a.m.
High Tide	3:02 p.m.	3:10 p.m.	3:19 p.m.	3:29 p.m.	3:40 p.m.

Activity 8b

Read on Target for Grade 6

Step 2 — Student Tips

To predict from the text, you need to remember:

- There are clues in the story. Clues are hints the author gives you about the story. Draw a line under each clue, or use your finger to point to the clue.

- What you know will help you make a guess about what will happen next in the story. Think about what is going on in the story. Have you done it before? Do you know about it?

- Clues, experiences, and knowledge are put together.

- Using clues from the story and what you know will help you figure out what will happen next. (This is called a **prediction**.)

Step 3 — Complete the reading map. Use the reading map to help you think about predicting.

Activity 8b   *Read on Target* **for Grade 6**

Map 8a

Infer from the Text

I read clues and use my knowledge to figure out what is happening in the story.

My Clues	+	My Experiences	=	My Prediction
Find clues in each sentence or paragraph that would help you answer the questions from the passage.		Think about your experiences and knowledge of a similar thing. Write your information in the boxes below.		Put the clues and experience/knowledge together to make a guess about what is happening in the story.
Clues about when Michael will surf.	→	Your experiences and knowledge of a similar thing.	→	When do you think Michael will surf?
Clues about when Jordan will collect seashells.	→	Your experiences and knowledge of a similar thing.	→	When do you think Jordan will collect seashells?
Clues that tell you what will happen if Michael surfs early in the morning.	→	Your experiences and knowledge of a similar thing.	→	What do you think will happen if Michael surfs early in the morning?

© 2006 Englefield & Associates, Inc.   COPYING IS PROHIBITED   53

Activity 8b Read on Target for Grade 6

Step 4 Read the following questions and write your answers.

1. Predict when high tide will be on Saturday. What clues helped you figure it out?

2. What time of the day on Sunday will Michael want to surf? How did you figure this out?

3. What would happen if Jordan decides to collect seashells next Monday at 5:30 p.m.?

4. What is the best time to collect seashells?

Activity 9a

Compare and Contrast
I read to find out how two or more things are alike and different.

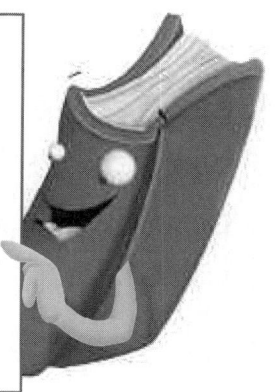

Step 1   Read the article "Frogs and Toads."

Frogs and Toads

It's important to look closely to see if the animal you are about to kiss is a frog or a toad. After all, a girl may never find a handsome prince if she kisses the wrong amphibian. Can you tell the difference between a frog and a toad?

At first glance, it may be easy to confuse frogs and toads. They are both amphibians. This means they can live both in water and on land. They both are coldblooded. This means their body temperatures are the same as the air temperature around them. They have to look for cool, shady places to rest if they become too hot. Frogs and toads look for warm, sunny places if they are too cold. Both animals are vertebrates, which means they have backbones. Their basic body shape is similar. Their eyes bulge out from their faces, so they can see in most directions without turning their heads. Frogs and toads use their long, sticky tongues to catch insects to eat. Both frogs and toads swallow their food whole.

© 2006 Englefield & Associates, Inc.   COPYING IS PROHIBITED   55

With all of these similarities, how are frogs and toads different? Frogs are better swimmers and jumpers, because they have long, muscular back legs. A toad's back legs are usually shorter. Frogs are more likely to be found near water, while toads often visit drier places. Most frogs have four webbed feet, but toads do not have webs on their back feet. The skin of a frog is smooth and slightly damp. Toads usually have drier skin that is covered with bumps called glands. Frogs have teeth in their upper jaw and rarely have teeth in their lower jaws. Toads have no teeth at all.

As you can see, frogs and toads are not the same amphibian. Of course, a frog turning into a handsome prince only happens in fairy tales. Who would want to kiss a frog or a toad anyway?

Activity 9a   *Read on Target* for Grade 6

Step 2 — Student Tips

To compare and contrast, you need to remember:

- You are looking at what is special about each thing. Think about what makes something special, like its color or its shape.

- You are checking out how things are alike and different. Compare means to tell how things are alike (the same). Contrast means to tell how things are different (not the same).

Step 3 — Complete the reading map. Use the reading map to help you think about comparing and contrasting.

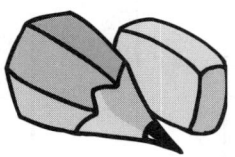

Activity 9a *Read on Target* for Grade 6

Map 9a

Compare and Contrast

I read to figure out how two things are alike and different.

Directions: How would you describe the things that you are going to compare and contrast? What shape are they? What color are they? Circle the plus sign (+) in a box if the items are similar. Circle the minus sign (–) in a box if the items are different.

Write the names of the things that you are going to compare and contrast in the two shaded boxes below.		
Describe the Characteristics. Tell what the things look like. Write your answer in the box next to these characteristics. (Under the shaded boxes.)		
Shape	+ or –	+ or –
Color	+ or –	+ or –
Size	+ or –	+ or –
It is. . .	+ or –	+ or –
Sounds like. . .	+ or –	+ or –
Feels like. . .	+ or –	+ or –
Write your own characteristic to compare and contrast.	+ or –	+ or –

© 2006 ENGLEFIELD & ASSOCIATES, Inc.   COPYING IS PROHIBITED

Activity 9a   Read on Target for Grade 6

Step 4
Read the following questions and write your answers.

1. Frogs and toads are what type of animal?

   _____

   _____

   _____

2. In what ways are frogs and toads different?

   _____

   _____

   _____

3. How are the body structures of frogs and toads alike?

   _____

   _____

   _____

4. Frogs and toads eat in a similar way. Identify this similarity.

   _____

   _____

   _____

Activity 9b

Compare and Contrast
I read to find out how two or more things are alike and different.

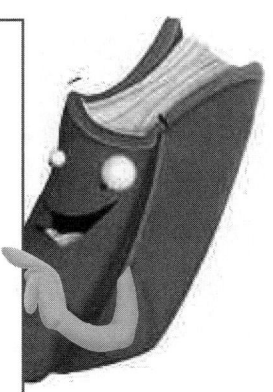

Step 1 Read the story "Apples and Oranges."

Apples and Oranges

My cousins Nikki and Logan are twins. You would think they would be just alike, but they are fraternal twins. That means although they were born at the same time, they do not share the exact same features. Twins who look exactly alike are called identical twins. We like to call Nikki and Logan "apples and oranges" because although they may be twins, they are not alike.

They do look a bit alike, considering that one is a boy and the other is a girl. They are both 5 feet tall. Their noses and mouths are the same shapes as their father's. Our grandmother used to call it an Irish lip. We never quite understood what that meant. Nikki has curly auburn hair and hazel eyes, and Logan has dark brown hair and very dark brown eyes. But their voices and facial expressions brand them as brother and sister, which they hate when people make mention of it.

When it comes to hobbies, that is where Nikki and Logan can really be called "apples and oranges." Nikki likes ballet and enjoys curling up alone with a good book. Logan, on the other hand, enjoys playing football and other sports. He enjoys spending his time with his friends outside. Nikki enjoys going to school, and her favorite part of school is art class. Logan does not like going to school. His favorite part of school is recess.

Nikki and Logan seem to fight constantly. When our family is together for holidays and special occasions, they always pick at and tease each other until the squawking becomes full blown. They always seem to end up "in the doghouse." I think the reason why they fight so much is they are competing for attention. Maybe it's because they are twins, and they have had to share a lot.

Activity 9b   **Read on Target for Grade 6**

One day on a family vacation, they were fighting so loudly, their parents came in from fishing out on the lake. Aunt Michelle and Uncle Dave said they could hear Nikki bellowing at Logan all the way out at their favorite perch hole. They came roaring in and told Nikki and Logan to go up to their rooms for the rest of the afternoon. We were all kind of sad because we had planned to have a water-basketball game and needed two more players to make up our teams. Nikki and Logan are both great water-basketball players. Neither one lets anyone get near the basket we have rigged up on the dock.

Nikki and Logan grudgingly left the dock, both blaming each other for getting themselves punished. Nikki slammed the door to the girls' bunkroom, and Logan did the same to the boys' side. We tried to get the water-basketball game under way without them, but it just wasn't the same without the two most aggressive players. Besides, we only had four people to play with instead of six. Finally, we called it quits and went up to the bunkrooms to get out of our wet bathing suits.

Nikki and Logan were in the girls' bunkroom talking and watching a movie together. When they saw us, Logan just smiled and Nikki grinned. I don't think they want us to know how much they really like each other. We just looked at each other, scratching our heads. I guess sometimes apples and oranges can come together to make a pretty good fruit salad!

© 2006 Englefield & Associates, Inc.   COPYING IS PROHIBITED   61

Activity 9b   Read on Target for Grade 6

Step 2 — **Student Tips**

To compare and contrast, you need to remember:

- You are looking at what is special about each thing. Think about what makes something special, like its color or its shape.

- You are checking out how things are alike and different. Compare means to tell how things are alike (the same). Contrast means to tell how things are different (not the same).

Step 3 — **Complete the reading map. Use the reading map to help you think about comparing and contrasting.**

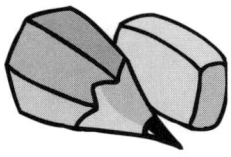

Activity 9b Read on Target for Grade 6

Map 9a

Compare and Contrast

I read to figure out how two things are alike and different.

Directions: How would you describe the things that you are going to compare and contrast? What shape are they? What color are they? Circle the plus sign (+) in a box if the items are similar. Circle the minus sign (−) in a box if the items are different.

Describe the Characteristics. Tell what the things look like. Write your answer in the box next to these characteristics. (Under the shaded boxes.)	Write the names of the things that you are going to compare and contrast in the two shaded boxes below.	
Shape		+ or −
Color		+ or −
Size		+ or −
It is . . .		+ or −
Sounds like . . .		+ or −
Feels like . . .		+ or −
Write your own characteristic to compare and contrast.		+ or −

© 2006 Englefield & Associates, Inc.   COPYING IS PROHIBITED

Activity 9b   *Read on Target* for Grade 6

Step 4 — Read the following questions and write your answers.

1. In the story, Nikki and Logan are twins. Tell some ways they are similar.

   _____

   _____

   _____

2. Explain some ways the twins are different.

   _____

   _____

   _____

3. Compare Logan and Nikki to other twins you have known. Are they similar to or different from other twins?

   _____

   _____

   _____

4. Decide whether you believe Logan and Nikki are more the same or more different. Give examples from the text to support your opinion.

   _____

   _____

   _____

Activity 10a

Analyze the Text by Examining the Use of Fact and Opinion

I figure out if the sentence can be proven or is a personal belief that tells how someone feels or thinks.

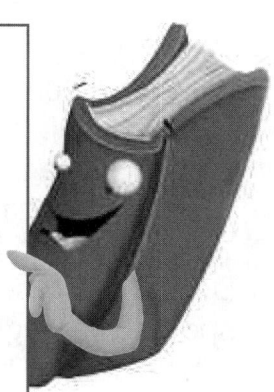

Step 1 Read the story "Washington, D.C."

Washington, D.C.

Our family went to Washington, D.C., for a week-long family trip at our nation's capital. Everyone loves Washington, D.C., because it is the only city in the United States that is not located in a state. I found it interesting that this city is the center of government in the United States. It is the capital of the United States. Washington, D.C., is a symbol of our country's history and tradition; consequently, it is a site of many popular tourist attractions.

The states of Maryland and Virginia border Washington, D.C. I saw the Potomac River to the west and south of the city. I was surprised to learn that this city is at least 69 square miles in size. Washington, D.C., seemed packed full of people. It is one of the more densely populated cities in the United States.

Some people go there to see senators, representatives, and, sometimes, the President. We were able to observe Congress in session. Watching government in action is exciting. This is the city where most of the federal employees work; thousands of people work in Washington, D.C. We were hoping to see the most important federal employee, the President.

Many people visit Washington, D.C. They go there to see government buildings, monuments, and other famous tourist attractions. Some of the sites I saw were the Lincoln Memorial, the Washington Monument, Ford's Theater, and the White House. We also visited a beautiful park with many blossoming cherry trees. Just imagine enjoying a large garden oasis right next to a bustling city.

The Lincoln Memorial is a stately white building that has a statue of President Abraham Lincoln sitting on a chair. Paintings and quotations from Lincoln were in the monument. It was very impressive. My favorite site, though, was the Washington Monument. When I went inside, I got on an elevator that whisked me to the very top. Because it is the tallest structure in Washington, D.C., I could see the whole city from the top of the monument. What a spectacular sight. After visiting the Washington Monument, we moved on to the White House. It was quite crowded but definitely worth the visit. I was able to tour several rooms such as the Red Room and the Blue Room with their magnificent works of art. At our last stop, Ford's Theater, we were able to tour the building where Abraham Lincoln was assassinated.

It was a busy week in Washington, D.C. I learned so much visiting various government sites. I think everyone would love to visit Washington, D.C., and would be fortunate to have an opportunity to visit our capital.

Activity 10a   *Read on Target* for Grade 6

Step 2   **Student Tips**

To analyze fact and opinion, you need to remember:

- **Facts** are true for everyone. They can be proven by seeing them or by looking them up.

- **Opinions** are true for some people. Opinions are beliefs about something. Some key words that let you know a sentence is an opinion are best, worst, bad, beautiful, ugly, always, never, everyone, mean, and kind.

- Read more about key words on the Fact and Opinion worksheet. Then, practice writing fact sentences and opinion sentences.

Step 3   **Complete the reading maps. Use the reading maps to help you think about facts and opinions.**

Activity 10a  Read on Target for Grade 6

Map 10a.1 — Analyze Aspects of the Text by Examining the Use of Fact and Opinion

I read to figure out if the reading is something that can be proven by evidence or if the reading is a personal belief that tells how someone feels or thinks about something.

Read a sentence from the story.

We also visited a beautiful park with many flowering cherry trees.

If you think the sentence is a FACT, then: ← **OR** → If you think the sentence is an OPINION, then:

If FACT	If OPINION
Write how the information that you read can be proven by evidence or observation. _____ _____ _____ Write where you would check by looking up the information or where you would see it. _____ _____ _____ Is the information true for everyone? _____	Write the KEY WORDS, which are clues that tell you how someone thinks, feels, or overstates. _____ _____ _____ Write how the information tells a personal belief or judgment about something. _____ _____ _____ Is the information true for some people? _____

68   COPYING IS PROHIBITED   © 2006 Englefield & Associates, Inc.

Activity 10a — **Read on Target for Grade 6**

Map 10a.2 — Analyze Aspects of the Text by Examining the Use of Fact and Opinion

I read to figure out if the reading is something that can be proven by evidence or if the reading is a personal belief that tells how someone feels or thinks about something.

Read a sentence from the story.

The city is at least 69 square miles.

← **OR** →

If you think the sentence is a FACT, then:

Write how the information that you read can be proven by evidence or observation.

_____
_____
_____

Write where you would check by looking up the information or where you would see it.

_____
_____
_____

Is the information true for everyone?

_____

If you think the sentence is an OPINION, then:

Write the KEY WORDS, which are clues that tell you how someone thinks, feels, or overstates.

_____
_____
_____

Write how the information tells a personal belief or judgment about something.

_____
_____
_____

Is the information true for some people?

_____

© 2006 Englefield & Associates, Inc.   COPYING IS PROHIBITED   69

Activity 10a  Read on Target for Grade 6

Map 10a.3 — Fact and Opinion Worksheet

Facts	Opinions
• true for everyone • can be proven and supported by evidence and observation • can be checked by looking up the information or seeing it	• true for some people • tells how someone thinks or feels about something • personal belief or judgment about something

You can use key words to change a fact into an opinion. Here are some examples of key words that will help you figure out if the information is an opinion.

KEY WORDS that describe an opinion:
best, great, easy, hard, beautiful, pretty, good, bad, difficult, ugly, terrible, excellent

KEY WORDS that overstate an opinion:
always, never, all, everyone

FACT + KEY WORD = OPINION

Here is an example: 1. This is a book. (fact) 2. This is a great book. (opinion)

Practice changing a fact into an opinion.

Read a fact sentence: The girl holds a dress.

Add a KEY WORD to change the fact into an opinion: _____

Practice changing an opinion into a fact.

Read an opinion sentence: My teacher always gives us difficult homework.

Take the KEY WORD out of the opinion sentence and write a fact sentence:

_____

Activity 10a *Read on Target* **for Grade 6**

Step 4
Read the following questions and write your answers.

1. List two facts from the text.

   _____

   _____

   _____

2. What is the author saying about Washington, D.C.?

   _____

   _____

   _____

3. The author mentioned the garden is beautiful. Is that a fact or an opinion? Explain your answer.

   _____

   _____

   _____

4. Tell why the author says everyone would love to visit Washington, D.C.

   _____

   _____

   _____

Activity 10b

Analyze the Text by Examining the Use of Fact and Opinion

I figure out if the sentence can be proven or is a personal belief that tells how someone feels or thinks.

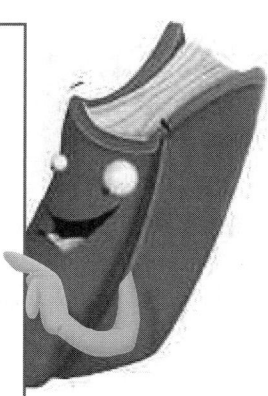

Step 1 Read the story "My Family Rendezvous."

My Family Rendezvous

I just had the best weekend of my life. My family went to a rendezvous encampment. Everyone at an encampment agrees to dress and to act as if they lived in another time period. Our rendezvous was planned to re-enact life on the Ohio frontier in the 1780s.

Just as people today need clothes to wear, people in the 1700s needed clothing to wear; however, what they wore and how they obtained their clothing back then is very different from today. When I outgrow my clothes, my family shops at a department store. There were no department stores on the Ohio frontier of 1780, so men and women had to make most of their own clothing. Therefore, most of the clothing worn at an encampment is made by hand. The men at the rendezvous wore pants made of animal hides. My stylish pants were made of beautiful deerskin that was the color of wheat and as soft as velvet. My dad paid for the deer hides with a check, and we sewed my pants by hand. It takes much more time to make your clothes by hand than it does to buy them at a store. In 1780, we probably would have had to hunt for the animals instead of buying the

72   COPYING IS PROHIBITED   © 2006 Englefield & Associates, Inc.

animal hides. If you weren't a good hunter, it could be a long time before you were able to make new pants or moccasins. Wearing jeans or gym shoes was not permitted at the rendezvous because they were invented after 1800.

Women of that time period wanted to be fashionable, just as all women today buy and wear the current fashions. In colonial days, women wore several long skirts or petticoats that hung to their ankles. Also, it was considered good manners for women and girls to wear some type of head covering all of the time, even to bed! Today some women wear hats for special occasions, but most women do not usually wear hats. Some women today wear T-shirts and shorts or pants, but women in the 1780s were not allowed to wear clothing that showed their elbows or legs. At the encampment, my mother wore a chemise (a long blouse), two brightly colored petticoats, a royal blue vest, and a snow-white hat called a mop cap. The mop cap had two rows of ruffles that framed her face. The ruffles shook like flower petals dancing in the wind when she laughed.

No one laughed during mealtime at the rendezvous. Cooking was serious work. It took a long time to prepare even one meal. Wood had to be chopped for the open fires where we cooked. We all had to be careful that our clothes did not brush against the flames or the coals of the cooking fire. I helped my dad carry water in canvas buckets from a nearby creek to our campsite for meals and safety in case something caught fire. The water was heavy, but since we were camping on a cool day, I hardly missed the running water we have at home. At the encampment, we cooked most of our food on a turning stick called a spit or in heavy black iron pots. There were no refrigerators, microwaves, electric stoves, or paper plates at the rendezvous or in the 1780s, but the food was just as delicious as if we had prepared the food at home.

Activity 10b Read on Target for Grade 6

Step 2 — Student Tips

To analyze fact and opinion, you need to remember:

- **Facts** are true for everyone. They can be proven by seeing them or by looking them up.

- **Opinions** are true for some people. Opinions are beliefs about something. Some key words that let you know a sentence is an opinion are best, worst, bad, beautiful, ugly, always, never, everyone, mean, and kind.

- Read more about key words on the Fact and Opinion worksheet. Then, practice writing fact sentences and opinion sentences.

Step 3 — Complete the reading maps. Use the reading maps to help you think about facts and opinions.

Activity 10b Read on Target for Grade 6

Map 10b.1 Analyze Aspects of the Text by Examining the Use of Fact and Opinion

I read to figure out if the reading is something that can be proven by evidence or if the reading is a personal belief that tells how someone feels or thinks about something.

Read a sentence from the story.

My stylish pants were made of beautiful deerskin that was a color of wheat and as soft as velvet.

← OR →

If you think the sentence is a FACT, then:	If you think the sentence is an OPINION, then:
Write how the information that you read can be proven by evidence or observation. _____ _____ _____ Write where you would check by looking up the information or where you would see it. _____ _____ _____ Is the information true for everyone? _____	Write the KEY WORDS, which are clues that tell you how someone thinks, feels, or overstates. _____ _____ _____ Write how the information tells a personal belief or judgment about something. _____ _____ _____ Is the information true for some people? _____

© 2006 Englefield & Associates, Inc.   COPYING IS PROHIBITED   75

Activity 10b   Read on Target for Grade 6

Map 10b.2 Analyze Aspects of the Text by Examining the Use of Fact and Opinion

I read to figure out if the reading is something that can be proven by evidence or if the reading is a personal belief that tells how someone feels or thinks about something.

Read a sentence from the story.

Wearing jeans or gym shoes was not permitted at the rendezvous because they were invented after 1800.

| If you think the sentence is a FACT, then: | ← OR → | If you think the sentence is an OPINION, then: |

FACT:
Write how the information that you read can be proven by evidence or observation.

_____
_____
_____

Write where you would check by looking up the information or where you would see it.

_____
_____
_____

Is the information true for everyone?

_____

OPINION:
Write the KEY WORDS, which are clues that tell you how someone thinks, feels, or overstates.

_____
_____
_____

Write how the information tells a personal belief or judgment about something.

_____
_____
_____

Is the information true for some people?

_____

Activity 10b   Read on Target for Grade 6

Map 10b.3 — Fact and Opinion Worksheet

Facts	Opinions
• true for everyone • can be proven and supported by evidence and observation • can be checked by looking up the information or seeing it	• true for some people • tells how someone thinks or feels about something • personal belief or judgment about something

You can use key words to change a fact into an opinion. Here are some examples of key words that will help you figure out if the information is an opinion.

KEY WORDS that describe an opinion:
best, great, easy, hard, beautiful, pretty, good, bad, difficult, ugly, terrible, excellent

KEY WORDS that overstate an opinion:
always, never, all, everyone

FACT + KEY WORD = OPINION

Here is an example: 1. This is a book. (fact) 2. This is a great book. (opinion)

Practice changing a fact into an opinion.

Read a fact sentence: I have a puppy.

Add a KEY WORD to change the fact into an opinion: _____

Practice changing an opinion into a fact.

Read an opinion sentence: Students always go to the football games.

Take the KEY WORD out of the opinion sentence and write a fact sentence:

_____

© 2006 Englefield & Associates, Inc.   COPYING IS PROHIBITED

Activity 10b   Read on Target for Grade 6

Step 4

Read the following questions and write your answers.

1. List three items from the text that, in your opinion, you would miss if you lived in the 1780s. Explain your opinions.

   _____

   _____

   _____

2. The author indicated that the rendezvous was the best weekend of his life. Find another opinion statement that describes another enjoyable aspect of the weekend.

   _____

   _____

   _____

3. What facts from the story might make someone choose to go camping at the rendezvous?

   _____

   _____

   _____

4. The author describes a different style of clothing for men and women of the 1780s. Give your opinion about how you would feel wearing similar clothing today.

   _____

   _____

   _____

Activity 11a

Explain How and Why an Author Uses Contents of a Text to Support His/Her Purpose for Writing

I tell the process (how) and the reason (why) the story was written.

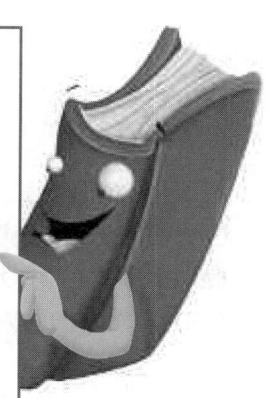

Step 1 Read the selection "The Constitution."

The Constitution

During a class trip to the library, Carlos and Juan were assigned a project to read and study information about the Constitution of the United States. They learned that the Constitution is our nation's basis for laws. They read that it established not only a group of independent states but a central form of government as well. It defined the powers of our government and established the protection of rights of all states and every person.

Juan and Carlos found out that after the Revolutionary War, our government was made up of an association of states. First, The Articles of Confederation were written. In it, our founding fathers established a national government, but they gave independence to each state and did not require states to work together to solve national problems. Carlos learned that the Constitution was written to develop a central government with three separate branches. Rules for trade between states and countries, as well as tax issues, were defined.

Juan said, "It was a good idea to write down something that tells what the responsibilities of our government are. I didn't realize how important it is to have a guide of basic laws that apply to all of the states."

Carlos said, "Those 13 states must have been a weak association back then, without any central government to hold them together."

"You know what?" said Juan, "I read that without the Constitution, there would be problems with providing money to support the government. Can you imagine a government being totally dependent on the states for money to operate? Without the permission of the states, the new government could not enforce laws, tax the states, or tax the people. Without a clear set of written

Activity 11a Read on Target for Grade 6

rules, each state acted like its own unique government—almost like an independent country. Each state could run its government just the way it wanted to."

Carlos replied, "To make matters worse, some people started thinking about revolting in order to solve their problems. The new government really needed something in writing!"

The boys' teacher, Mrs. Thompson, heard Juan and Carlos' discussion and stopped by their table. Mrs. Thompson explained to them that there are also specific powers defined in the Constitution. Some of the federal powers included the right to collect taxes, to declare war, and to regulate trade. Other powers were left to the states and reserved for the people.

"In my opinion," Mrs. Thompson said, "one very important power reserved for the people is the right to own property." She also told them, "Although many powers are defined as separate, you will see that in some cases, the federal government and the states have the ability to act at both federal and state levels."

Mrs. Thompson then explained, "The Constitution has a preamble, seven articles, and twenty-seven amendments. It basically sets up a system that divides powers between the federal (central government) and the states. It also established a balance by setting up three branches of government: the executive branch, the legislative branch, and the judicial branch. The executive branch enforces the laws; the legislative branch makes the laws; the judicial branch interprets the laws. Thus, we have three separate branches that can check and balance one another. This is known as the separation of powers."

"I get it!" Juan exclaimed. "That really makes sense! No one part of the government can ever become too powerful. I think everyone should know why the constitution was written. Without it, we would not have the type of government, rules, freedoms, and rights we have today. The Constitution is a really important document."

Activity 11a *Read on Target* for Grade 6

Step 2 — Student Tips

To explain the author's purpose for writing, you need to remember:

- Tell why. "Why" is the reason the author wrote the text.
- Tell how. Find words or pictures that help you figure out the author's process for writing.
- Look for clues that tell you why authors write:

  Enjoyment (Funny sentences, interesting words, and images)

  Understand (Words that tell you what people (characters) are like and what they think, feel, or do)

  Find Out/Learn (Facts, charts, graphs, and pictures)

  Solve Problems (Words that tell you about an action or a decision)

  Persuade (Words that tell you how you should think)

Step 3 — Complete the reading map. Use the reading map to help you think about the author's purpose for writing.

Activity 11a

Read on Target for Grade 6

Map 11a — Explain How and Why an Author Uses Contents of a Text to Support His/Her Purpose for Writing

I tell the process (how) and the reason (why) the story was written.

Purpose of Fiction	Purpose of Poetry	Purpose of Nonfiction
• enjoyment and entertainment • understand life, people, and experiences • find out about the lives of the characters and how they are similar to you • understand how characters solve problems that may be similar to yours	• enjoyment of the poet's feelings • expressive words and images • understand the poet's thoughts about life • find out about the subject • solve problems in your life by comparing them to the poet's writing	• enjoyment • understand something • give information, facts, or data • help you solve problems • figure out how to do something • persuade you to agree with the author

Circle the type of writing.	Tell why the story was written by writing the author's purpose for the story. (Pick an answer from the purpose boxes.)
fiction poetry nonfiction	

Write sentences from the text that show how the author tells the purpose for writing.

_____

_____

_____

© 2006 Englefield & Associates, Inc.

Activity 11a   Read on Target for Grade 6

Step 4
Read the following questions and write your answers.

1. What is the author's purpose for writing this sentence: "The Constitution has a preamble, seven articles, and twenty-seven amendments. It basically sets up a system that divides powers between the federal (central government) and the states"?

   _____
   _____
   _____

2. What is the author's purpose for writing this sentence: " Mrs. Thompson explained to them that there are also specific powers defined in the Constitution"?

   _____
   _____
   _____

3. What type of writing is this text?

   _____
   _____
   _____

4. Write a sentence from the text that has factual information that helps the reader understand the author's purpose.

   _____
   _____
   _____

© 2006 Englefield & Associates, Inc.   COPYING IS PROHIBITED   83

Activity 11b

Explain How and Why an Author Uses Contents of a Text to Support His/Her Purpose for Writing

I tell the process (how) and the reason (why) the story was written.

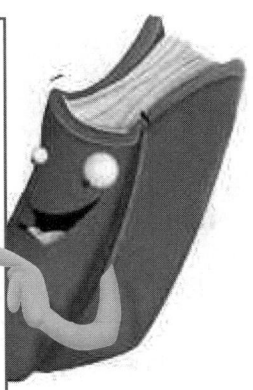

Step 1 Read the announcement "Drama Club Meeting."

Drama Club Meeting

Attention All Meridian Middle School Students

A membership meeting for the Meridian Middle School Drama Club will be held Monday, September 19, in the media center from 3:00 p.m. to 4:00 p.m. Come meet current members of our club to find out how much fun it is to be a thespian. The Drama Club is open to all middle school students.

We need all kinds of people to be in Drama Club.

- People with desire to be on stage such as actors, comics, singers, and dancers—we need you. Come and entertain your peers.

- People who like to work off stage—we need you. We can teach you how to be a prop manager, a screen technician, a lighting technician, and a sound technician.

- People who are creative and artistic—we need you. Backdrop artists, costume designers, and cover designers are needed.

- People who like to work with computers—we need you. Help print our programs or control the special effects graphics.

- There is a place for everyone who wants to join Drama Club.

This year's production is "Middle School Madness."

We meet Monday and Thursday of every week from 3:00 p.m. to 4:00 p.m.

Sign up on the bulletin board in the cafeteria, and show up in the media center on Monday. You should come because you will have fun. Free refreshments will be served. See you there!

Activity 11b   *Read on Target* for Grade 6

Step 2 — Student Tips

To explain the author's purpose for writing, you need to remember:

- Tell why. "Why" is the reason the author wrote the text.
- Tell how. Find words or pictures that help you figure out the author's process for writing.
- Look for clues that tell you why authors write:

    Enjoyment (Funny sentences, interesting words, and images)

    Understand (Words that tell you what people (characters) are like and what they think, feel, or do)

    Find Out/Learn (Facts, charts, graphs, and pictures)

    Solve Problems (Words that tell you about an action or a decision)

    Persuade (Words that tell you how you should think)

Step 3 — Complete the reading map. Use the reading map to help you think about the author's purpose for writing.

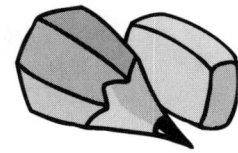

Activity 11b   *Read on Target for Grade 6*

Map 11b — Explain How and Why an Author Uses Contents of a Text to Support His/Her Purpose for Writing

I tell the process (how) and the reason (why) the story was written.

Purpose of Fiction	Purpose of Poetry	Purpose of Nonfiction
• enjoyment and entertainment • understand life, people, and experiences • find out about the lives of the characters and how they are similar to you • understand how characters solve problems that may be similar to yours	• enjoyment of the poet's feelings • expressive words and images • understand the poet's thoughts about life • find out about the subject • solve problems in your life by comparing them to the poet's writing	• enjoyment • understand something • give information, facts, or data • help you solve problems • figure out how to do something • persuade you to agree with the author

Circle the type of writing.	Tell why the story was written by writing the author's purpose for the story. (Pick an answer from the purpose boxes.)
fiction poetry nonfiction	

Write sentences from the text that show how the author tells the purpose for writing.

_____

_____

_____

Activity 11b

Read on Target for Grade 6

Step 4 — Read the following questions and write your answers.

1. How did you determine the author's purpose for writing the announcement?

   _____
   _____
   _____

2. How did the author try to persuade you to attend the meeting?

   _____
   _____
   _____

3. If the author's purpose was changed to **enjoyment**, how would the announcement be different?

   _____
   _____
   _____

4. Do you think the announcement is successful in achieving its purpose? Why or why not?

   _____
   _____
   _____

Activity 12a

Evaluate and Critique the Text for Organizational Structure

I discuss whether the reading flows from idea to idea and why the organization is a strength or a weakness.

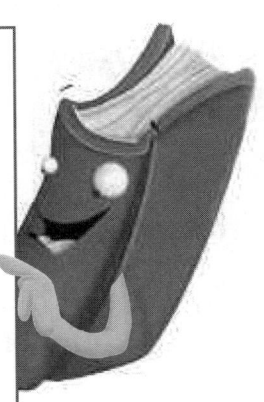

Step 1 Read the poem "Happy Birthday, U.S.A."

Happy Birthday, U.S.A.

July 4th, 1776—In Philadelphia, a day to rejoice,
Our founding fathers raised a voice.
The Declaration of Independence,
Signed by one and all from this day hence.

Bands played,
Contests, games, and food were made.
People laughed, danced, and sang,
While all the bells of freedom rang.

Today—The tradition continues from year to year,
As we remember what we all hold dear.
Our democracy, freedom, rights, laws
Are remembered by one and all.

Our parades, picnics, and fireworks are a clue,
And symbolize our freedom—red, white, and blue.
Yes, parties, fun, and festivities are a way,
To celebrate this special day.

Activity 12a ***Read on Target* for Grade 6**

Step 2 — Student Tips

To help you understand whether the text flows from idea to idea and why the organizational structure of the text is a strength or a weakness, you need to remember:

- There are four basic ways an author organizes the writing.
  Time order (chronological)
  Cause and effect order (links what happened and why it happened)
  Order of importance (information given in the text is ordered from least important to most important or vice versa)
  Compare and contrast order (looks at how information is alike or different from other information)
- To think about whether the way the information is presented is clear or confusing
- To consider whether the author's organization kept you interested in or excited about the information or whether it made the information seem boring
- To see if you were able to follow the sequence of information or if it was difficult for you to follow
- There can be more than one type of order within a single text

Step 3 — Complete the reading map. Use the reading map to help you think about evaluating and critiquing the text for organizational structure.

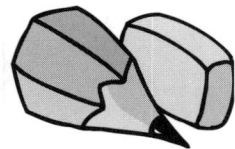

Activity 12a Read on Target for Grade 6

Map 12a

Evaluate and Critique the Text for Organizational Structure

I discuss whether the reading flows from idea to idea and why it is a strength or a weakness.

Time Order: The ideas are in the order that they occur from earliest to latest or latest to earliest.

Cause and Effect Order: The author shows how an action causes something to happen.

Order of Importance: The ideas start from most important to least important or from least important to most important.

Compare and Contrast Order: All the ideas that are alike may be discussed first. Next, all of the ideas that are different are discussed. Or, each idea may be compared and contrasted.

The strengths are...

The type or types of organization used by this author is . . . (Choose from the four boxes above.)

Here are some ways that the organization is strong or weak (effective or not effective).

The weaknesses are...

How effective is the organization of the article or the paragraph that you read? Why?

Activity 12a   *Read on Target* **for Grade 6**

Step 4
Read the following questions and write your answers.

1. What two types of organizational structures do you think the author used? How did you arrive at your answer?

   _____

   _____

   _____

2. How did the organizational structure help you understand the information presented in the text?

   _____

   _____

   _____

3. We celebrate the Fourth of July in a different way than it was celebrated in 1776. Give an example to support this.

   _____

   _____

   _____

4. Why do you think people in the U.S.A. celebrate the Fourth of July?

   _____

   _____

Activity 12b

Evaluate and Critique the Text for Organizational Structure

I discuss whether the reading flows from idea to idea and why the organization is a strength or a weakness.

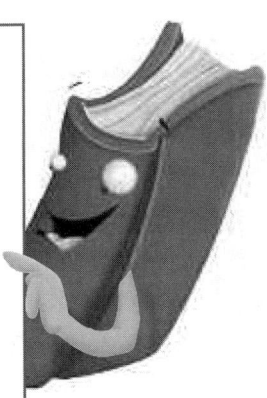

Step 1 Read the story "Cliff Jumping."

Cliff Jumping

For as long as I could remember, I had heard my dad's and my uncle's stories about jumping off the cliffs into a lake in Canada. I never really thought much about it except that they must have been crazy or exaggerating, or both. They used to brag about climbing cliffs that were 30 feet tall and jumping into the water below that was over 80 feet deep. Who would do anything so silly?

One year, we went on vacation to that very same lake, Lake Manitou. When my dad first launched our boat, I said jokingly, "Hey, Dad, how about taking us to the cliffs?" I expected him to take us to a big rock on shore and say something like, "Well, it used to seem much bigger when we were kids."

As we sped along over the clear blue water, the shore began to change from low, rocky outcroppings, to ledges that became higher and higher. They were pine-covered, with some of the pines actually growing out of the faces of the cliffs. Sometimes, there would be tall ledges that jutted out over the lake, but there were rocks in the water below, as if there had once been an earthquake that had shaken them loose from their rocky homes. I was sure my dad and uncle had been telling tales as tall as those cliffs. Jumping off those cliffs looked dangerous.

Then we rounded the next bluff; we saw boats anchored in the water just off shore. Dad slowed the boat and cut the engine. We could hear laughter and shouts of excitement and encouragement. There, cut into the rock shore by Mother Nature herself, was a perfectly smooth right angle cliff that rose into the air about 30 feet. The water lapped gently at the high smooth wall. The water was a deep, deep green that seemed to hint at the depth below. My dad threw out the 100-foot anchor line, and it disappeared right up to where it was tied to the boat.

Kids and adults were climbing up a steep rock face a short way down the shore. They were holding a rope tied to some trees; it helped them scale the rocks. Some people were perched on a lower ledge that jutted out of the smooth face of the cliff like a balcony on a house, while some scrambled all the way to the top. As I watched, you could see every single climber pause as he or she looked from the top of the cliff into the water below. Some people jumped quickly as if they just wanted to get it over with. Their screams of excitement rang out as they plunged into the water. The scene made me want to try it and to run away at the same time. Others stayed at the top for what seemed like forever. You could tell they wanted to jump but just couldn't. I understood exactly how they felt.

Did I dare try it? Dad seemed to understand. He said, "Come on, Lauren, I will, if you will." As if something were drawing me to insanity, I jumped over the side of the boat into the water and swam to shore. I dragged myself up those rocky cliffs holding onto the rope as if it was my link to heaven. Did I mention that I am afraid of heights? As I climbed out on the ledge, I held onto a nearby pine tree. I looked over the edge to see the same frightening sight all those others had seen. What was I doing up on this ledge? Such things are for adventure seekers only.

Suddenly from behind, Dad took my hand and said, "Come on, Lauren, you'll love it." I ignored the voice in my head that kept telling me I was too scared to jump. "On the count of three," Dad said enthusiastically. I held my breath and jumped. It seemed as if I would never reach the water. The air rushed by me as my heart seemed to pound through my chest. Then whoosh, into the cold depths, we kept going down, down, down. I began to wonder if I had enough air to get back up to the surface. As my head broke back into the sunlight, I gasped. I did it! I was in one piece, alive, and I had jumped. My dad was laughing and gasping for air just like I was.

I wonder what my children will think someday about my story of jumping off a cliff. I know one thing for sure—there will only be one story, because I won't be doing it again.

Activity 12b   Read on Target for Grade 6

Step 2   **Student Tips**

To help you understand whether the text flows from idea to idea and why the organizational structure of the text is a strength or a weakness, you need to remember:

- There are four basic ways an author organizes the writing.

  Time order (chronological)

  Cause and effect order (links what happened and why it happened)

  Order of importance (information given in the text is ordered from least important to most important or vice versa)

  Compare and contrast order (looks at how information is alike or different from other information)

- To think about whether the way the information is presented is clear or confusing

- To consider whether the author's organization kept you interested in or excited about the information or whether it made the information seem boring

- To see if you were able to follow the sequence of information or if it was difficult for you to follow

- There can be more than one type of order within a single text

Step 3   Complete the reading map. Use the reading map to help you think about evaluating and critiquing the text for organizational structure.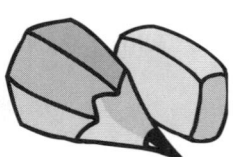

Activity 12b *Read on Target* for Grade 6

Map 12b — Evaluate and Critique the Text for Organizational Structure

I discuss whether the reading flows from idea to idea and why it is a strength or a weakness.

Time Order:	Cause and Effect Order:	Order of Importance:	Compare and Contrast Order:
The ideas are in the order that they occur from earliest to latest or latest to earliest.	The author shows how an action causes something to happen.	The ideas start from most important to least important or from least important to most important.	All the ideas that are alike may be discussed first. Next, all of the ideas that are different are discussed. Or, each idea may be compared and contrasted.

The type or types of organization used by this author is . . . . (Choose from the four boxes above.)
_____
_____

Here are some ways that the organization is strong or weak (effective or not effective).

↑ **The weaknesses are. . .**
_____
_____
_____
_____

↓ **The strengths are. . .**
_____
_____
_____
_____

How effective is the organization of the article or the paragraph that you read? Why?
_____
_____

© 2006 ENGLEFIELD & ASSOCIATES, Inc.   COPYING IS PROHIBITED   95

Activity 12b   Read on Target for Grade 6

Step 4 **Read the following questions and write your answers.**

1. What type of organizational structure did the author use?

___

2. What words in the text gave you information as to how the author organized the information?

___

3. What details did the author include to help make this story seem organized?

___

4. How else could the author have ended the story?

___

Activity 13a

Evaluate and Critique the Text for Logic and Reasoning

I tell if the reading is backed up by reasons and evidence.

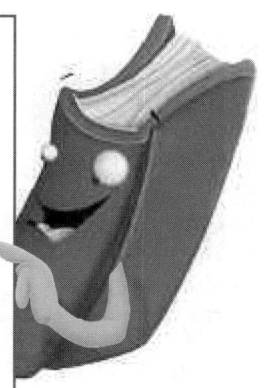

Step 1 Read the article "Help Scientists Study the Ecosystem."

Help Scientists Study the Ecosystem

Some scientists study the ecosystem. An ecosystem includes groups of living and non-living things that interact with one another. Scientists know that ecosystems can vary in size. They can be as small as a puddle or as large as the planet Earth. Temperature, light, food, and population density are some of the factors that make up an ecosystem.

Ongoing studies focus on how changing one or more of the ecosystem factors impacts the entire ecosystem. For example, a fire in Yellowstone National Park completely changed the nature of the system. There are no longer large trees, moss, or large bushes. After a short time, small grass, shrubs, and flowers grew. The small vulnerable animals had to move to a different place to survive. The loss of so much beauty and wildlife saddened the whole country.

It is the opinion of many people that fires can be devastating. Many scientists think there should be a quicker response time to put out forest fires. They also think more money needs to be spent on protecting the environment. After seeing displaced animals, many people in the community feel the same way. Lobbying efforts are in place to provide additional money for studying the ecosystem.

Scientists will continue to study the impact of natural events on the environment. Their work is a valuable asset to all; however, money is desperately needed to continue to study ecosystems. If you would like to contribute financial support, please send your check or money order to a local organization. You never know what plants or animals you might be saving.

Activity 13a   *Read on Target* for Grade 6

Step 2 — Student Tips

To help you evaluate and critique the text for logic and reasoning, you need to remember:

- Logic and reasoning skills are similar to determining fact and opinion.
- Use the left side of the reading map to list the information that is backed up with facts, reasons, or evidence.
- Use the right side of the reading map to list the information that includes feelings, emotions, or opinions.
- **Completing the chart in the reading map will show you the balance of the argument.**
- This reading map helps you recognize persuasive text and helps you to not be influenced by persuasive feelings. It also helps you recognize texts that are more factual and are backed by reasons and evidence.

Step 3

Complete the reading map. Use the reading map to help you think about evaluating and critiquing for logic and reasoning.

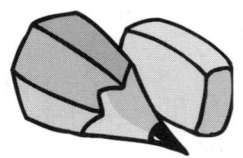

Activity 13a

Read on Target for Grade 6

Evaluate and Critique the Text for Logic and Reasoning

I tell if the reading is backed up by reasons and evidence.

Map 13a

STRENGTHS
List the facts, reasons, and evidence in the text.

WEAKNESSES
List the feelings, emotions, and opinions in the text.

Here is what the author wants me to believe:

Here is the information that tells if the reading is backed by facts or feelings.

Does the information rely more on facts or feelings? _____

Is the information biased? _____

Does the text have enough facts, evidence, and reasoning to support the information? _____

Activity 13a   Read on Target for Grade 6

Step 4 — Read the following questions and write your answers.

1. How do fires affect the ecosystem?

   _____
   _____
   _____

2. What are some advantages of contributing to the study of the ecosystem?

   _____
   _____
   _____

3. How do scientists feel about the importance of studying the ecosystem?

   _____
   _____
   _____

4. Why did the author add opinions and feeling statements to the text?

   _____
   _____
   _____

Activity 13b

Evaluate and Critique the Text for Logic and Reasoning

I tell if the reading is backed up by reasons and evidence.

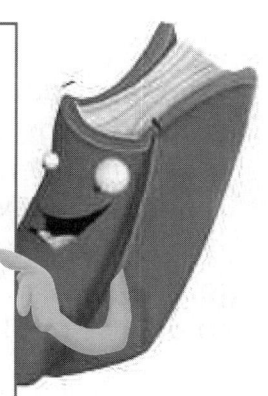

Step 1 Read the story "Who is Right?"

Who Is Right?

Joelle's brother Mark was just about to turn sixteen. One day he came home from school extremely upset. He had just heard that the state legislature was going to raise the driving age to eighteen.

"That is just totally stupid," complained Mark. "Just when I get to drive, those adults in the legislature want to ruin it for me!"

Joelle was only twelve, but she understood how much Mark was looking forward to getting his license. She was hoping he could take her friends and her around to all the places they wanted to go. Mark had told her he would drive her places when he got his license. All she had to do was wash the car for him once a month. It seemed like a reasonable trade-off to Joelle. A car wash was definitely worth having rides to the mall and to the movies.

Joelle heard her mother explaining insurance statistics to Mark. The legislators had been using this information to support their new bill. She said almost 75 percent of sixteen-year-old drivers have an accident.

Mark retorted, "Maybe 75 percent of eighteen-year-old drivers would have accidents, too, because it's inexperience, not age, that makes the difference."

Joelle thought about that and decided it made sense. In fact, it was the first thing that Mark had said that afternoon that really made sense to her.

Joelle's mother continued, "Legislators feel sixteen-year-old kids are just too reckless. They don't think about the consequences of their actions. And I have to agree with them."

Mark answered, "Mom, how can you generalize like that? You're stereotyping people. Maybe some sixteen year olds are like that, but so are some eighteen year olds. Believe it or not, there are also some really responsible sixteen year olds. Think about this: how am I going to get a job if I don't have a way to get there? I can't save money for college if I don't have a job. For every reason those legislators give for not permitting sixteen year olds to drive, I bet I have a reason they should."

His mother looked at him thoughtfully, but she didn't say anything. Mark continued, "I also wanted to join the Big Brother program. I thought I would make a great mentor. But I can't do anything like that if I don't have a way to get there. Besides, Dad says we need to watch our money, and I could be a big help if I had my license and could get a job."

"I don't suppose the legislators thought about that, but more about safety issues," answered his mother. "Maybe I'll call our congressman's office and give him my opinions."

"You know, Mom, I think I will, too," declared Mark.

Joelle just looked at them, thinking about all they had said. Then she thought, "I sure hope I can drive when I am sixteen. Maybe I'll call the congressman's office, too."

Activity 13b   *Read on Target* for Grade 6

Step 2 — Student Tips

To help you evaluate and critique the text for logic and reasoning, you need to remember:

- Logic and reasoning skills are similar to determining fact and opinion.

- Use the left side of the reading map to list the information that is backed up with facts, reasons, or evidence.

- Use the right side of the reading map to list the information that includes feelings, emotions, or opinions.

- **Completing the chart in the reading map will show you the balance of the argument.**

- This reading map helps you recognize persuasive text and helps you to not be influenced by persuasive feelings. It also helps you recognize texts that are more factual and are backed by reasons and evidence.

Step 3 — Complete the reading map. Use the reading map to help you think about evaluating and critiquing for logic and reasoning.

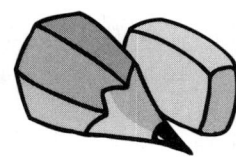

© 2006 Englefield & Associates, Inc.   COPYING IS PROHIBITED   103

Activity 13b *Read on Target* for Grade 6

Map 13b

Evaluate and Critique the Text for Logic and Reasoning
I tell if the reading is backed up by reasons and evidence.

STRENGTHS
List the facts, reasons, and evidence in the text.

Here is what the author wants me to believe:

Here is the information that tells if the reading is backed by facts or feelings.

WEAKNESSES
List the feelings, emotions, and opinions in the text.

Does the information rely more on facts or feelings? _____

Is the information biased? _____

Does the text have enough facts, evidence, and reasoning to support the information? _____

104 COPYING IS PROHIBITED © 2006 ENGLEFIELD & ASSOCIATES, INC.

Activity 13b   *Read on Target* **for Grade 6**

Step 4

Read the following questions and write your answers.

1. What are the strengths of Mark's argument?

   _____
   _____
   _____

2. How do the legislators' opinions differ from Mark's?

   _____
   _____
   _____

3. When Mark calls his congressman, what do you think he should or should not say?

   _____
   _____
   _____

4. Do you agree with Mark or with the legislators? Why?

   _____
   _____
   _____

Activity 14a

Evaluate and Critique the Text
I tell about the strengths and weaknesses of what I read.

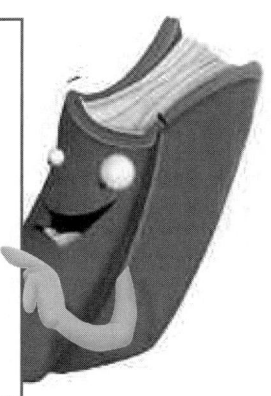

Step 1 Read the story "George."

George

George is everybody's friend. He never thinks of anyone as a stranger, and he talks to everyone he meets. He talks with people in the grocery store and at the gas station. George is the kind of person who people are attracted to because of his outgoing personality. He is sincere and kind. He is honest and compassionate.

George is about six feet tall with a large body frame accentuated by strong arms and a broad chest. His balding head retains some of the gray, short hair around the sides. In his younger days, his hair was somewhat curly. His hazel eyes are concealed slightly by glasses. His beard is graying to match his hair color, reflective of older age. His beard and hair looked better when they were brown. He looked more like his brother Stephen, but now Stephen's hair is still brown and George's is gray.

All of his life, George has helped others. As a pharmacist, he gave advice to people when they were sick, and he made sure they knew what to do to feel better quickly. He checked to make sure they understood his directions. He assisted people with household tasks, too. He helped carry furniture when people moved. He cleaned up when basements flooded. There was almost no job he wouldn't do. He believed that helping people was important in life.

In addition to helping people, George listened to them. He wanted to hear what they said. He listened to stories about work, and he listened to stories about family life. The more he listened, the more people shared with him. He thought that listening to others showed them what they had to say was important, and he believed it was.

Now that George is a grandfather, he continues to help and listen. He listens to young voices telling him important thoughts about how to play dominoes and matching games. He listens to the children's mother when she is concerned about their health and safety. He offers free advice, and it is usually accurate. He helps with his strong arms, tenderly lifting his baby grandchild out of the crib and into his lap while he reads a favorite story in his special way.

I have seen how George demonstrates his kindness and compassion. So many times he has shown his sincerity and genuine concern. He is a man anyone would be proud and lucky to know.

Activity 14a   *Read on Target* for Grade 6

Step 2: Student Tips

To evaluate and critique the text, you need to remember:

- List the strengths (good points) and the weaknesses (bad points).
- See if the information agrees with the question. Ask yourself, "Does this information agree with the question? Does this information not agree with the question?"
- Tell why you think the answer is right.

Step 3

Complete the reading map. Use the reading map to help you think about evaluating and critiquing the text.

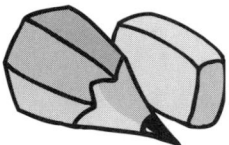

Activity 14a   *Read on Target* for Grade 6

Map 14a   Evaluate and Critique the Text
I tell about the strengths and the
weaknesses of what I read.

Did the author make you think it would be good to have George as a friend?

The strengths are...	The weaknesses are...
_____	_____
_____	_____
_____	_____
_____	_____
_____	_____
_____	_____
_____	_____

After reading the strengths and weaknesses, the answer to the question is:
_____
_____
_____
_____

© 2006 Englefield & Associates, Inc.   COPYING IS PROHIBITED

Activity 14a *Read on Target* **for Grade 6**

Step 4
Read the following questions and write your answers.

1. Write one reason why having George as a friend would be good.

    _____
    _____
    _____

2. Write another reason why having George as a friend would be good.

    _____
    _____
    _____

3. Write one reason why having George as a friend would not be good.

    _____
    _____
    _____

4. Do you think that having George as a friend would be a good idea or a bad idea?

    _____
    _____
    _____

Activity 14b

Evaluate and Critique the Text
I tell about the strengths and weaknesses of what I read.

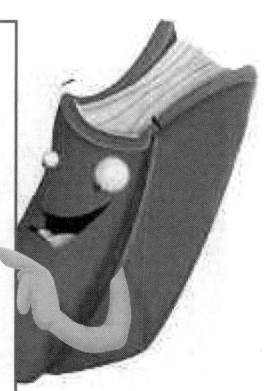

 **Step 1** Read the article "The Survey."

The Survey

In this day and age of nutritional awareness regarding calorie intake, types of vitamins, and benefits of food and drink, scientists wanted to find out which types of drinks people preferred. They felt that by providing health and nutrition information, they would influence the preference of people toward a particular type of drink.

As a result, 50 people were given a questionnaire. This form provided information regarding calorie value and health and nutritional information of four different types of drinks. The respondents were asked to rate their preferences for the different types of drinks by rating their favorites. After completion, they were given a coupon to choose one free bottle of diet soda pop, orange juice, regular soda pop, or water. Study the chart on the next page before answering the questions.

Activity 14b   *Read on Target* for Grade 6

Type of Drink	Calories per Bottle	Information from the Warnings/Benefits Label	Percent Rated as Favorite Drink
Diet Soda Pop	0	"Great Taste" "Contains Aspartame (some people may be allergic to phenylalanine, an ingredient in aspartame)"	35%
Water	0	"Helps Regulate Body Temperature"	25%
Regular Soda Pop	100	"Tastes Good"	30%
Orange Juice	110	"A Good Source of Vitamin C and Vitamin D" "Great Natural Taste"	10%

Activity 14b *Read on Target* for Grade 6

Step 2 — Student Tips

To evaluate and critique the text, you need to remember:

- List the strengths (good points) and the weaknesses (bad points).
- See if the information agrees with the question. Ask yourself, "Does this information agree with the question? Does this information not agree with the question?"
- Tell why you think the answer is right.

Step 3

Complete the reading map. Use the reading map to help you think about evaluating and critiquing the text.

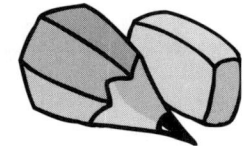

Activity 14b   Read on Target for Grade 6

Map 14b Evaluate and Critique the Text
I tell about the strengths and the weaknesses of what I read.

Did the author give you enough information to choose which drink is healthiest for you?

The strengths are...

The weaknesses are...

After reading the strengths and weaknesses, the answer to the question is:

Activity 14b   Read on Target for Grade 6

Step 4 Read the following questions and write your answers.

1. Which drink has the most calories per bottle?

   _____
   _____
   _____

2. Why do you think diet soda has the highest rating?

   _____
   _____
   _____

3. If you were running a race, which drink would you choose? Why?

   _____
   _____
   _____

4. Present an argument for not using artificial sweeteners such as aspartame.

   _____
   _____
   _____

Activity 15a

Summarize the Text

I tell the overall meaning of the story in my own words.

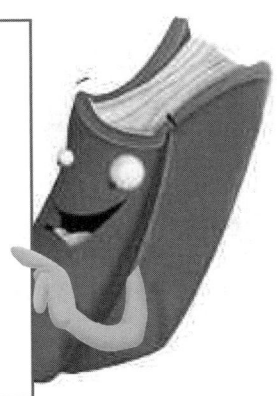

Step 1 Read the article "Beavers of North America."

Beavers of North America

Beavers are furry mammals with teeth that are a distinguishing characteristic. They have two sets of teeth. In front, beavers have four orange-enameled sharp teeth that they use to chop down trees. Beavers also use their teeth to peel bark and cut branches. These front teeth continue to grow and to wear down as the beavers chew and chop wood. In addition to strong front teeth, beavers have 16 teeth in the back of their mouths for chewing. Their teeth help them survive in their environment.

Beavers can be found in North America. Many live in the United States near rivers, streams, ponds, lakes, and woods. They usually weigh about 30 pounds, but some beavers can weigh as much as 70 pounds. An average-sized beaver is approximately 30 inches long. Beavers use their teeth and strong jaw muscles to build lodges and dams. These lodges look like tepee-shaped piles of sticks and logs. The beavers put the sticks and logs together using layers of mud, sticks, and rocks. Because the beaver is a very social animal, several beaver families often occupy a single lodge.

A beaver dam is built near the lodge. The dam makes the water around the lodge deeper so beavers can swim under the lodge to get inside. These ten-foot-long dams can stand as tall as five feet high. They are built from sticks, poles, and solidly packed mud, brush, and stones. As time goes by, repairs are often needed to preserve the strength and effectiveness of the dams.

Beavers are industrious mammals that are interesting to study. The beavers continuously work hard, chopping down new trees to maintain their dams and lodges. They are always busy cutting and building. Perhaps this is why we say a hardworking person is "busy as a beaver."

Activity 15a   *Read on Target* for Grade 6

Step 2 — Student Tips

To summarize the text you need to remember:

- Each paragraph has a main idea. Tell only the important information in each paragraph. Leave out unimportant information. Use your own words (different words that mean the same thing as the words in the story). Make sure you stay on topic.

- You should follow these steps.

    1. Read the whole text.
    2. Next, read one paragraph at a time.
    3. Circle important information. This will help you know what to write on your reading map.
    4. Write one sentence that tells the main idea of each paragraph in your own words.
    5. Last, write the overall idea of the whole text in your own words.

Step 3 — Complete the reading maps. Use the reading maps to help you think about summarizing the text.

© 2006 Englefield & Associates, Inc.   COPYING IS PROHIBITED   117

Activity 15a Read on Target for Grade 6

Map 15a.1

Summarize the Text
I tell the overall meaning of what I read in my own words.

Summary Sentences
Cross out the unimportant information from paragraph 1.
Circle the most important details.

Beavers are furry mammals with teeth that are a distinguishing characteristic. They have two sets of teeth. In front, beavers have four orange-enameled sharp teeth that they use to chop down trees. Beavers also use their teeth to peel bark and cut branches. These front teeth continue to grow and to wear down as the beavers chew and chop wood. In addition to strong front teeth, beavers have 16 teeth in the back of their mouths for chewing. Their teeth help them survive in their environment.

Think about the most important information that you circled. Now, use your own words to write one sentence that tells the overall idea of the paragraph.

_____

_____

_____

_____

Activity 15a   *Read on Target* for Grade 6

Map 15a.2

Summarize the Text
I tell the overall meaning of what I read in my own words.

Summary Sentences
Cross out the unimportant information from paragraph 2. Circle the most important details.

Beavers can be found in North America. Many live in the United States near rivers, streams, ponds, lakes, and woods. They usually weigh about 30 pounds, but some beavers can weigh as much as 70 pounds. An average-sized beaver is approximately 30 inches long. Beavers use their teeth and strong jaw muscles to build lodges and dams. These lodges look like tepee-shaped piles of sticks and logs. The beavers put the sticks and logs together using layers of mud, sticks, and rocks. Because the beaver is a very social animal, several beaver families often occupy a single lodge.

Think about the most important information that you circled. Now, use your own words to write one sentence that tells the overall idea of the paragraph.

_____
_____
_____
_____

Activity 15a   **Read on Target** for Grade 6

Map 15a.3

Summarize the Text
I tell the overall meaning of what I read
in my own words.

Summary Sentences
Cross out the unimportant information from paragraph 3.
Circle the most important details.

A beaver dam is built near the lodge. The dam makes the water around the lodge deeper so beavers can swim under the lodge to get inside. These ten-foot-long dams can stand as tall as five feet high. They are built from sticks, poles, and solidly packed mud, brush, and stones. As time goes by, repairs are often needed to preserve the strength and effectiveness of the dams.

Think about the most important information that you circled. Now, use your own words to write one sentence that tells the overall idea of the paragraph.

_____
_____
_____
_____

Activity 15a Read on Target for Grade 6

Map 15a.4

Summarize the Text
I tell the overall meaning of what I read in my own words.

Summary Sentences
Cross out the unimportant information from paragraph 4.
Circle the most important details.

Beavers are industrious mammals that are interesting to study. The beavers continuously work hard, chopping down new trees to maintain their dams and lodges. They are always busy cutting and building. Perhaps this is why we say a hardworking person is "busy as a beaver."

Think about the most important information that you circled. Now, use your own words to write one sentence that tells the overall idea of the paragraph.

_____

_____

_____

_____

© 2006 Englefield & Associates, Inc.   COPYING IS PROHIBITED

Activity 15a Read on Target for Grade 6

Map 15a.5

Summarize the Text
I tell the overall meaning of what I read in my own words.

Use your own words to write one sentence that tells the overall idea of the entire text.

_____
_____
_____
_____
_____
_____

Activity 15a Read on Target for Grade 6

Step 4
Read the following questions and write your answers.

1. Write one detail from the first paragraph that tells about beavers' teeth.

   _____

   _____

   _____

2. Write a summary sentence for the first paragraph.

   _____

   _____

   _____

3. Write a summary sentence for the third paragraph that tells about the beaver dam.

   _____

   _____

   _____

4. Write one sentence to summarize the entire text.

   _____

   _____

   _____

Activity 15b

Summarize the Text
I tell the overall meaning of the story in my own words.

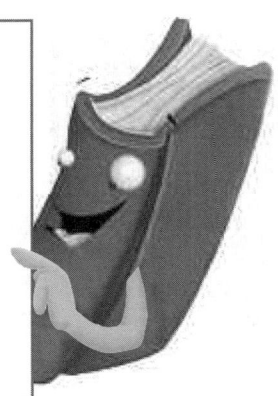

Step 1
Read the article "Bottle-Nosed Dolphins."

Bottle-Nosed Dolphins

Bottle-nosed dolphins are sea animals that live in salt water. The name "bottle-nosed" comes from the shape of the animal's snout. The slightly turned-up curve of the mouth, plus the shape of the nose, gives the bottle-nosed dolphin the appearance of always smiling. Many people say they look like friendly pets. In addition to the bottle nose, the unique shape of the dolphin's dorsal fin makes the animal easy to identify.

Bottle-nosed dolphins are marine mammals; that is, they are warm-blooded animals that live in water. Although they swim in waters of varying temperatures, the dolphin's body temperature remains the same. These playful dolphins breathe air through a blowhole on the top of their heads. Like other mammals, baby dolphins drink milk from their mothers. A female dolphin may care for a dolphin calf until it is 18 months old.

Dolphins are intelligent animals. The brains of dolphins and of humans are about the same size. Dolphins navigate through the water by making clicking sounds. When the dolphins send out these high-pitched noises through the water, those sounds bounce off objects in the water. From the echoes, the bottle-nosed dolphin is able to detect the size and location of those objects in the water. Researchers are often interested in studying the dolphin's ability to locate even the smallest object from a far distance.

Marine biologists have learned many things about dolphins by watching them in captivity. There is still much to learn and many questions to answer about these intelligent and friendly-looking mammals.

Activity 15b Read on Target for Grade 6

Step 2

Student Tips

To summarize the text you need to remember:

- Each paragraph has a main idea. Tell only the important information in each paragraph. Leave out unimportant information. Use your own words (different words that mean the same thing as the words in the story). Make sure you stay on topic.

- You should follow these steps.

    1. Read the whole text.

    2. Next, read one paragraph at a time.

    3. Circle important information. This will help you know what to write on your reading map.

    4. Write one sentence that tells the main idea of each paragraph in your own words.

    5. Last, write the overall idea of the whole text in your own words.

Step 3

Complete the reading map. Use the reading map to help you think about summarizing the text.

© 2006 Englefield & Associates, Inc.　　COPYING IS PROHIBITED

Activity 15b Read on Target for Grade 6

Map 15b.1

Summarize the Text
I tell the overall meaning of what I read in my own words.

Summary Sentences
Cross out the unimportant information from paragraph 1.
Circle the most important details.

Bottle-nosed dolphins are sea animals that live in salt water. The name "bottle-nosed" comes from the shape of the animal's snout. The slightly turned-up curve of the mouth, plus the shape of the nose, gives the bottle-nosed dolphin the appearance of always smiling. Many people say they look like friendly pets. In addition to the bottle nose, the unique shape of the dolphin's dorsal fin makes the animal easy to identify.

Think about the most important information that you circled. Now, use your own words to write one sentence that tells the overall idea of the paragraph.

_____
_____
_____
_____

Activity 15b Read on Target for Grade 6

Map 15b.2

Summarize the Text
I tell the overall meaning of what I read in my own words.

Summary Sentences
Cross out the unimportant information from paragraph 2.
Circle the most important details.

Bottle-nosed dolphins are marine mammals; that is, they are warm-blooded animals that live in water. Although they swim in waters of varying temperatures, the dolphin's body temperature remains the same. These playful dolphins breathe air through a blowhole on the top of their heads. Like other mammals, baby dolphins drink milk from their mothers. A female dolphin may care for a dolphin calf until it is 18 months old.

⬇   ⬇

Think about the most important information that you circled. Now, use your own words to write one sentence that tells the overall idea of the paragraph.

_____

_____

_____

_____

Activity 15b   Read on Target for Grade 6

Map 15b.3

Summarize the Text
I tell the overall meaning of what I read in my own words.

Summary Sentences
Cross out the unimportant information from paragraph 3.
Circle the most important details.

Dolphins are intelligent animals. The brains of dolphins and of humans are about the same size. Dolphins navigate through the water by making clicking sounds. When the dolphins send out these high-pitched noises through the water, those sounds bounce off objects in the water. From the echoes, the bottle-nosed dolphin is able to detect the size and location of those objects in the water. Researchers are often interested in studying the dolphin's ability to locate even the smallest object from a far distance.

Think about the most important information that you circled. Now, use your own words to write one sentence that tells the overall idea of the paragraph.

_____
_____
_____
_____

Activity 15b Read on Target for Grade 6

Map 15b.4

Summarize the Text
I tell the overall meaning of what I read in my own words.

Summary Sentences
Cross out the unimportant information from paragraph 4.
Circle the most important details.

Marine biologists have learned many things about dolphins by watching them in captivity. There is still much to learn and many questions to answer about these intelligent and friendly-looking mammals.

Think about the most important information that you circled. Now, use your own words to write one sentence that tells the overall idea of the paragraph.

_____

_____

_____

_____

Activity 15b Read on Target for Grade 6

Map 15b.5

Summarize the Text
I tell the overall meaning of what I read in my own words.

Use your own words to write one sentence that tells the overall idea of the entire text.

Activity 15b   Read on Target for Grade 6

Step 4

Read the following questions and write your answers.

1. Write a summary sentence from the first paragraph telling why the bottle-nosed dolphins were given their name.

   _____

   _____

   _____

2. Write two details that tell you how bottle-nosed dolphins are able to navigate in the ocean without bumping into things.

   _____

   _____

   _____

3. Write two details that tell you why bottle-nosed dolphins are mammals.

   _____

   _____

   _____

4. Write one sentence to summarize the entire text.

   _____

   _____

   _____

Activity 16a

Identify Cause and Effect
I read to find out the reason why something happened and what happened.

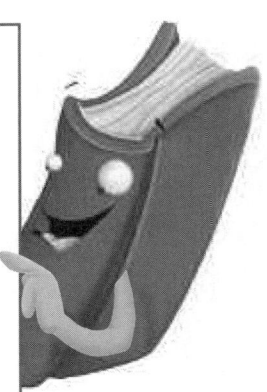

Step 1 Read the article "A Balloon Ride."

A Balloon Ride

Have you ever wondered how people use a large balloon to fly in the air? It is quite amazing to see a large colorful balloon high up in the sky. Hot air balloons seem almost magical, but they are really large bags filled with hot air. Balloons have a basket attached so that people can take rides. The baskets are suspended below the balloon. People are able to stand in the basket; they can look around as the balloon lifts off the ground.

You might wonder how the balloon is able to rise with people holding it down. But the hot air behaves in a special way. When air is heated, it warms the air molecules. These molecules start to move faster and faster. The warm molecules push each other and take up more space. As the air continues to heat, the molecules speed up and push harder against each other. The expanded air takes up more space than the cold air. Because the air inside the balloon has expanded, the balloon inflates, increasing in volume.

The hot air that fills the inside of the balloon has fewer molecules than the colder air outside the balloon. Consequently, the hot air weighs less. The balloon rises because the hot air molecules are lighter and weigh less. The balloon pushes up, up, up into the air, high in the sky. As people riding in the basket float up in the sky, they can see many sights below. Farms, houses, trees, and people all seem smaller as the balloon floats away.

Activity 16a **Read on Target for Grade 6**

    When it is time to land, the air is slowly cooled, and the exact opposite process happens. When the air inside the balloon is cooled, its molecules slow down. They lose energy and take up less space. Cooling the air results in the balloon deflating and losing volume. The air continues to be cooled slowly, so the balloon can sink lower to the ground. Finally, the air is cooled to the point that the balloon contracts. The balloon ride is over as the basket sinks to the ground, but the experience will stay with the balloonists for a long time, all because of hot air!

Activity 16a   *Read on Target* for Grade 6

Step 2: Student Tips

To identify cause and effect, you need to remember:

- The **cause** is the action or the reason that makes something happen (why something happened).

- The **effect** is the result (what happened).

- Look for key words that are clues to help you figure out if the statement is a cause or an effect.

    - Some of the key words that tell you why something happened (cause) are: **because**, **since**.

    - Some of the key words that tell you what happened (effect) are: **therefore**, **as a result**.

Example Sentences

Here is an example of a cause and effect sentence:

- **Because** gold was discovered in the west (cause), many people moved to the west to get wealthy (effect).

Sometimes the order is reversed and the effect comes before the cause. Here is an example of an effect and cause sentence:

- Many people moved to the west (effect) **because** gold was discovered (cause).

Step 3: Complete the reading map. Use the reading map to help you think about cause and effect.

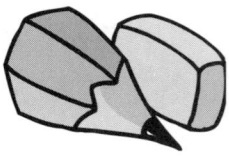

Activity 16a Read on Target for Grade 6

Map 16a

Identify Cause and Effect
I read to find out the reason why something happened and what happened.

The air in the balloon takes up more space

Cause: **Why** something happened (Reason/Action)

→ As a result →

Effect: **What** happened (result)

The balloon rises

Effect: **What** happened (result)

→ Because →

Cause: **Why** something happened (Reason/Action)

© 2006 Englefield & Associates, Inc.   COPYING IS PROHIBITED   135

Activity 16a   **Read on Target** for Grade 6

Step 4
Read the following questions and write your answers.

1. What causes the balloon to deflate?

   _____

   _____

   _____

2. Why does the balloon gain volume and expand?

   _____

   _____

   _____

3. Why does the hot air in the balloon weigh less?

   _____

   _____

   _____

4. If the temperature of the balloon is the same as the air outside of the balloon, what happens to the balloon?

   _____

   _____

   _____

Activity 16b

Identify Cause and Effect
I read to find out the reason why something happened and what happened.

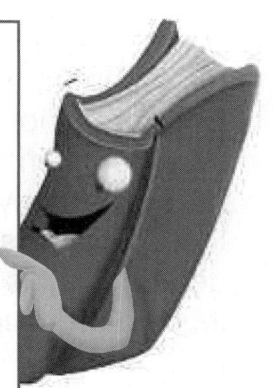

Step 1 Read the article "Glaciers in Our World."

Glaciers in Our World

Massive, huge, and unusual is how I described the glacier that I saw. As I stood there, shivering underneath my parka, I couldn't believe my eyes. Glaciers are large, ever-drifting masses of ice found in cold regions high in the mountains. The snow builds up quickly, more quickly than it melts. As the snow grows deeper, it compacts and turns to ice.

The glacier I saw was in Switzerland. I spotted it in a valley between two mountains. I think it ranged from 600 feet to 1,000 feet in depth. This valley glacier was extremely thick ice with a long, narrow body that filled high in between the mountains. Its ice was so deep and cold that it appeared deep blue in some spots.

I watched the glacier as our tour guide began to explain how glaciers shaped the land. During the Ice Age, glaciers covered a large part of our world. As glaciers moved across the land, they impacted the land's features, creating a variety of landforms. They were powerful forces, moving and changing the terrain. After the Ice Age was over, the glaciers melted and left behind large holes filled with water. I saw evidence of this as I looked down the mountain; ponds and lake formations were nestled in the mountains, and deposits of bedrock, clay, and sand had been left behind in the valleys.

I couldn't wait to get home. For one thing, I was pretty cold, but I also wanted to do some more research on this amazing natural wonder. I started with an Internet search. I was amazed at the history behind these awesome formations. One of the articles I read said glaciers existed 10,000 years ago. As my tour guide had said, glaciers covered large areas of our world back then.

Activity 16b   **Read on Target** for Grade 6

I learned many other interesting facts about glaciers. Glaciers begin to form when the snow falls. In Switzerland, this happens during the long winter in the mountains. In the spring, the snow gradually melts leaving excess water, which refreezes. As you can imagine, the frozen water becomes ice. This ice packs on top of itself. As a result, the ice becomes heavy and compacted, turning into dense crystals of ice. The ice becomes so thick and heavy that it moves under its own pressure. Glaciers are sometimes referred to as "rivers of ice."

How interesting it is to see what happened to our world as a result of glaciers moving across the land! Perhaps you will have an opportunity to study the land formations in your area and discover the effect the glaciers have had.

GLACIER

Activity 16b   Read on Target for Grade 6

Step 2 — **Student Tips**

To identify cause and effect, you need to remember:

- The **cause** is the action or the reason that makes something happen (why something happened).

- The **effect** is the result (what happened).

- Look for key words that are clues to help you figure out if the statement is a cause or an effect.

    - Some of the key words that tell you why something happened (cause) are: **because**, **since**.

    - Some of the key words that tell you what happened (effect) are: **therefore**, **as a result**.

Example Sentences

Here is an example of a cause and effect sentence:

- **Because** gold was discovered in the west (cause), many people moved to the west to get wealthy (effect).

Sometimes the order is reversed and the effect comes before the cause. Here is an example of an effect and cause sentence:

- Many people moved to the west (effect) **because** gold was discovered (cause).

Step 3 — Complete the reading map. Use the reading map to help you think about cause and effect.

Activity 16b   *Read on Target* **for Grade 6**

Map 16b

Identify Cause and Effect

I read to find out the reason why something happened and what happened.

Cause: Why something happened (Reason/Action)

During the Ice Age, glaciers moved across the land

As a result

Effect: What happened (result)

Effect: What happened (result)

Effect: What happened (result)

140   COPYING IS PROHIBITED   © 2006 Englefield & Associates, Inc.

Activity 16b   Read on Target for Grade 6

Step 4: Read the following questions and write your answers.

1. What causes glaciers to move across the land?

   _____
   _____
   _____

2. What causes the dense crystals of ice?

   _____
   _____
   _____

3. How are ponds formed?

   _____
   _____
   _____

4. How do you think a group of large lakes, such as the Great Lakes, might have been formed?

   _____
   _____
   _____

Activity 16c

Identify Cause and Effect
I read to find out the reason why something happened and what happened.

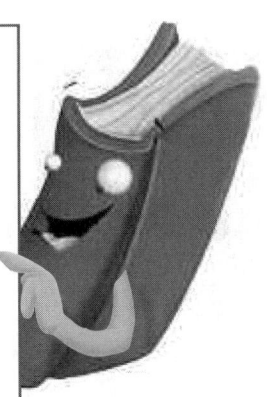

Step 1 Read the article "The Biggest Wave."

The Biggest Wave

Every so often, incredibly huge waves move in the ocean. They have enormous speed and intensity. These immense, swift-moving waves are called tidal waves or tsunamis. Tsunamis are more common in the Pacific Ocean than anywhere else on Earth.

Scientists are researching the causes of tsunamis. They have found that tsunamis can be the result of a sudden drop in part of the ocean floor. They can also be caused by underwater landslides or earthquakes. Such land movements under the ocean can cause a tremendous underwater wave. At first, the wave looks like a small ripple. However, the wave gains power and force as it continues toward the shore. It then becomes a dangerous, fast-moving wave of lightning speed and unimaginable power.

Many people have seen incredible destruction brought about by this dangerous tidal wave. As the waves go barreling to the shore, they crash into anything in their way. Tsunamis can smash houses, trees, and anything else in their paths.

Since scientists have no way of knowing how often an underwater disturbance that could create a tsunami will occur, it is important to start mapping the floor of the ocean. The ocean floor is covered with underwater mountains and trenches. Earthquakes, landslides, and other sudden drops of the ocean floor are important events that scientists are working hard to discover more about. As scientists conduct research into the causes of tsunamis, they should be able to predict the occurrence of these tidal waves. That way, people can be warned, find safety, and protect their belongings before the tsunamis arrive.

Activity 16c   Read on Target for Grade 6

Step 2 — **Student Tips**

To identify cause and effect, you need to remember:

- The **cause** is the action or the reason that makes something happen (why something happened).
- The **effect** is the result (what happened).
- Look for key words that are clues to help you figure out if the statement is a cause or an effect.
    - Some of the key words that tell you why something happened (cause) are: **because**, **since**.
    - Some of the key words that tell you what happened (effect) are: **therefore**, **as a result**.

Example Sentences

Here is an example of a cause and effect sentence:

- **Because** gold was discovered in the west (cause), many people moved to the west to get wealthy (effect).

Sometimes the order is reversed and the effect comes before the cause. Here is an example of an effect and cause sentence:

- Many people moved to the west (effect) **because** gold was discovered (cause).

Step 3 — Complete the reading map. Use the reading map to help you think about cause and effect.

Activity 16c

Read on Target for Grade 6

Map 16c

Identify Cause and Effect

I read to find out the reason why something happened and what happened.

Tsunamis happen

Effect: **What** happened (result)

Because

Cause: **Why** something happened (Reason/Action)

Cause: **Why** something happened (Reason/Action)

Cause: **Why** something happened (Reason/Action)

Activity 16c

Read on Target for Grade 6

Step 4

Read the following questions and write your answers.

1. Tsunamis are more common in the Pacific Ocean. Name a state that might be affected by tsunamis. (Note: You may need to use a map.)

   _____

   _____

   _____

2. Why is a tsunami dangerous?

   _____

   _____

   _____

3. What kinds of destruction do tsunamis cause?

   _____

   _____

   _____

4. Why do scientists hope to learn more about when tsunamis occur?

   _____

   _____

   _____

Self-Scoring Chart

Self-Scoring Chart

Rate how well you understand the critical-thinking steps by putting a star (★) for mastery, a plus sign (+) for making progress, and a minus sign (−) for needs help. You can rate what you know four different times.

Characters	1	2	3	4
Name a character				
Match sentences with the descriptions of the character				
Tell how the character impacts the story				
Tell how the story would be different if you changed a characteristic of the character				

Setting	1	2	3	4
Describe the setting: Tell where the story takes place				
Describe the setting: Tell when the story takes place				
Describe the setting: Tell what the setting looks like				
Tell how the setting affects the characters				
Tell how the setting affects the events				
Change the setting: Change where the story takes place				
Change the setting: Change when the story takes place				
Change the setting: Change what the setting looks like				
Tell how the characters would be different if the setting changed				
Tell how the events would be different if the setting changed				

Plot	1	2	3	4
Describe the chain of events by writing the major events in correct order				
Change the plot by choosing an event to happen earlier or later				
Tell how the story is different when one of the events has been changed				
Take an event out of the story				
Tell what would be different if one of the events is left out of the story				
Write what would happen if the character's actions were different				

Self-Scoring Chart

Read on Target for Grade 6

Problem/Solution	1	2	3	4
Know the definition of a problem and a solution				
Write the problem of the story you read				
Write the events that lead up to the solution				
Write the solution of the story				
Write a different problem by making up your own problem				
Write how the events would be different if the problem changed				
Write how the solution would be different if the problem changed				

Point of View	1	2	3	4
Know the definition and key word pronouns of each point of view				
Identify the point of view in the story				
Write sentences from the story that helped you figure out the point of view				
Tell why the author writes from the point of view				
Tell how changing the point of view would affect the story				

Theme	1	2	3	4
Name some ideas from the text that tell what the story is about				
Write the lessons that the character learned				
Write a sentence telling what the message of the story is				

Infer	1	2	3	4
Read each sentence/paragraph to find clues about the story's meaning				
Write a clue in the clue box				
Write about an experience or knowledge you have of a similar thing				
Put the clue and your experience or knowledge together to make an inference about what is happening in the story				
Read more of the story to see if the inference is correct				

© 2006 Englefield & Associates, Inc.   COPYING IS PROHIBITED

Self-Scoring Chart

Read on Target for Grade 6

	1	2	3	4
Predict				
Read each sentence/paragraph to find clues about the story's meaning				
Write a clue in the clue box				
Write about an experience or knowledge you have of a similar thing				
Put the clue and your experience or knowledge together to make a prediction about what will happen next				
Read more of the story to see if the prediction is correct				

	1	2	3	4
Compare and Contrast				
Write the names of the things to be compared and contrasted				
Describe the characteristics				
If the items have same characteristics, mark them with a plus sign				
If the items have different characteristics, mark them with a minus sign				

	1	2	3	4
Fact and Opinion				
Write sentences that tell you if the text is a fact or an opinion				
Write how the information can be proven by evidence or observation				
Write where you would look up information to check it				
Tell if the information is true for everyone				
Write key words that are clues to tell how someone thinks or feels				
Write how the information tells a personal belief or judgment				
Tell if the information is true for some people				

	1	2	3	4
Explain Purpose for Writing				
Know the definitions and purposes of fiction, poetry, and nonfiction				
Identify the type of writing				
Write the author's purpose				
Write a sentence or sentences from the story that show an example of the author's purpose				

Self-Scoring Chart

Read on Target for Grade 6

	1	2	3	4
Evaluate and Critique the Text for Organizational Structure				
Know the definitions of the types of organizational structure				
Write the types of organizational structure used				
List some ways the organization is a strength or a weakness				
Write how effective the organization is and why				

	1	2	3	4
Evaluate and Critique the Text for Logic and Reasoning				
Write what the author wants you to think or believe				
List the sentences that contain facts, reasons, or evidence				
List the sentences that contain feelings, emotions, or opinions				
Determine if the information if biased				
Determine if the information has enough evidence to support the author's belief				

	1	2	3	4
Evaluate and Critique the Text				
Read the question given by the teacher				
List the strengths of the text				
List the weaknesses of the text				
After reading the strengths and weaknesses, answer the question				

	1	2	3	4
Summarize the Text				
Circle the important information from each paragraph				
Rewrite the important information in each paragraph using your own words				
Use your own words to tell the overall idea of the whole selection				

	1	2	3	4
Identify Cause and Effect				
Know the definitions of cause and effect				
Read the key words for cause and effect				
Write why something happened (the cause)				
Write what happened (the effect)				

© 2006 Englefield & Associates, Inc.   COPYING IS PROHIBITED

Notes

Notes

Subject-Specific Skill Development
Workbooks Increase Testing Skills

Write on Target for grades 1/2, 3, 4, 5, and 6

Includes Graphic Organizers

Read on Target for grades 1/2, 3, 4, 5, and 6

Includes Reading Maps

Math on Target for grades 3, 4, and 5

Includes Thinking Maps

For more information, call our toll-free number: 1.877.PASSING (727.7464)
or visit our website: www.showwhatyouknowpublishing.com